ENTERPRISE AI CONTROL

HOW ORGANIZATIONS GOVERN INTELLIGENT SYSTEMS AT SCALE

GOVIND PATHAK

notionpress.com

INDIA • SINGAPORE • MALAYSIA

ISBN
Paperback 979-8-90479-890-1
Hardcase 979-8-90510-273-8

Disclaimer

The views, frameworks, and opinions in this book are solely those of the author and are intended for educational, informational, and thought leadership purposes only. They do not constitute legal, regulatory, financial, investment, or compliance advice of any kind.

This book does not constitute:

- Legal or regulatory advice
- Financial or investment advice
- Compliance certification
- Cybersecurity assurance
- Engineering implementation guarantee

Readers are responsible for:

- Evaluating risks and ensuring compliance
- Verifying applicability to their organization
- Consulting qualified legal, regulatory, and technical professionals
- Implementing appropriate safeguards before deployment

Evolving Landscape

AI technologies, regulations, and governance practices change rapidly. References, frameworks, and examples in this book may evolve over time.

Conceptual Frameworks

Models including the Four-Layer Control Model, AI Control Maturity Model, and Runtime Guardrails are strategic in nature and require organizational adaptation.

No Endorsement

References to companies, products, standards, or industries are strictly illustrative and imply no endorsement, criticism, or official affiliation.

Independent Views

The author's observations are shared independently and do not reflect the views of current or former employers, clients, industry bodies, or regulatory authorities.

⚠ The author and publisher shall not be held liable for direct or indirect losses, operational failures, security incidents, compliance violations, financial damages, or business interruptions arising from the application of concepts discussed in this book.

Final Note: This book is written with the belief that Artificial Intelligence represents one of the most transformative technologies of our time. Its purpose is not to discourage innovation, but to encourage responsible, controlled, and accountable innovation.

"The future of AI will not depend only on what systems can do but on how responsibly humanity chooses to design, govern, and control them."

PREFACE

AI CONTROL: From Intelligence to Accountable Systems

By Govind Pathak

We are entering a defining moment in technological history. AI systems are no longer simply assisting human decisions; they are increasingly **making decisions themselves.** As AI capability accelerates, one critical dimension remains underdeveloped: **control.** This book addresses the widening gap between intelligence and responsibility, speed and oversight, optimization and human intent.

The Shift: From Automation to Autonomous Decision Systems

Across industries, AI is no longer a tool it is becoming **the decision layer of infrastructure.** This transformation demands a fundamental rethinking of how organizations govern the systems they deploy.

Financial Services

Approving transactions, detecting fraud, and managing regulated AI ecosystems at scale.

Telecom

Optimizing networks and controlling critical infrastructure through autonomous operations.

Enterprise Operations

Managing supply chains, influencing customer behavior, and executing autonomous workflows.

Healthcare

Prioritizing clinical interventions and supporting decisions that directly affect human lives.

> **"Organizations were becoming increasingly capable of deploying AI, but insufficiently prepared to govern how these systems make decisions at scale."**
> Govind Pathak

The Gap That Emerged

- Policies existed, but enforcement did not
- Monitoring existed, but intervention did not
- Automation existed, but accountability did not

The Competitive Frontier Has Shifted

Companies will no longer compete solely on data, models, or automation speed. The decisive advantage will belong to organizations that demonstrate **trust, control, and accountability** in their AI systems. The most powerful AI will not win the most **controlled** AI will.

A Framework for Governed AI

This book introduces a practical and strategic framework for building AI systems that can be **trusted, audited, and governed** from decision boundaries to full lifecycle control.

1

Policy

Defining the rules and intent that govern how AI systems are permitted to act.

2

Process

Embedding governance into workflows, escalation paths, and operational rhythms.

3

Enforcement

Runtime guardrails, kill switches, and control mechanisms that operate at the system level.

4

Interface

Observability, auditability, and human-facing controls that maintain meaningful oversight.

> ⓘ A central argument of this book: **Governance without enforcement is incomplete.** Policies alone do not control AI systems. Only systems designed with embedded control mechanisms can do that.

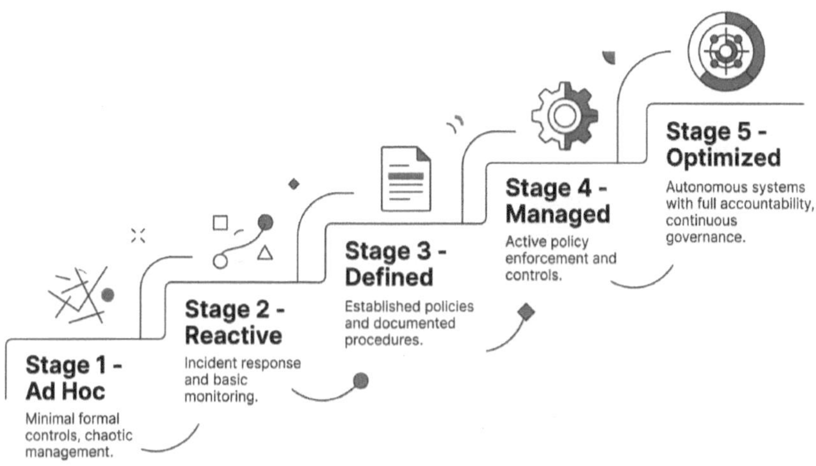

The AI Control Maturity Model helps organizations assess where they stand and chart a responsible path forward through decision boundaries, third-party AI governance, and controlled autonomy frameworks.

Who This Book Is For

- CTOs, CIOs, and technology executives
- AI architects and engineers
- Governance, risk, and compliance professionals
- Policymakers and transformation leaders

The Final Principle

> **"The true measure of intelligence is not only the ability to act. It is the ability to know when not to act."** Govind Pathak

The next era of technology will belong to systems that understand boundaries, accountability, permission, and responsibility systems that remain aligned with human intent even as they act autonomously.

WHY THIS BOOK MATTERS

AI Control: From Intelligence to Accountable Systems

We are deploying AI into the most critical systems of our era: telecom networks, financial infrastructure, and security operations at a scale and speed that has outpaced our governance models. **This book addresses the gap between how we govern AI and how AI actually works.** The future will not be defined by intelligence alone. It will be defined by control.

Why This Book Matters Now

AI systems today operate continuously, in real time, and at massive scale. In many deployments, humans are no longer directly approving every action decisions are increasingly autonomous, and optimization is quietly overriding human intent. Yet our governance response remains largely document-driven: policies, guidelines, compliance reviews.

⚠ **The core problem is simple:** Policies do not control systems. Systems control systems.

Critical Infrastructure at Risk

AI is embedded in telecom networks, financial systems, security infrastructure, and enterprise workflows operating without human approval at every step.

Autonomous Without Accountability

Decisions are increasingly autonomous. Optimization is overriding human intent. The systems act but there is no embedded mechanism for accountability.

Governance Still Paper-Based

Most organizations respond with documents policies, audits, and reviews that have no direct connection to how the systems actually behave at runtime.

This book addresses that gap by introducing a new discipline: **the architecture of AI control** embedded directly into the systems themselves.

The Core Premise: From Intelligent to Accountable

> If AI can decide, it must also know when *not* to decide.

What Makes This Book Different

Unlike traditional AI books focused on machine learning techniques or data science, this book focuses on **the architecture of AI control**. It introduces practical frameworks designed for technical leaders and enterprise architects:

Four-Layer Control Model

Structural framework for embedding control across AI system layers

AI Control Maturity Model

Assess and advance your organization's control posture over time

Runtime Guardrails

Boundaries that enforce behavior dynamically not just at design time

Controlled Autonomy Frameworks

Enable AI to act with speed while preserving human oversight and intent

The Enterprise Transition

Old World	Emerging World
Human-led decisions	AI-driven decisions
Static systems	Adaptive systems
Workflow automation	Autonomous execution
Governance documents	Runtime control systems

Organizations that fail to establish control mechanisms will face AI drift, misaligned automation, regulatory pressure, and trust deficits.

This book combines technology, governance, risk management, enterprise architecture, and leadership strategy into a unified, control-centric approach positioning AI control not as a compliance exercise, but as **a strategic capability for the autonomous era**.

Epilogue: The Final Boundary

> The true measure of intelligence is not simply the ability to act. It is the ability to act responsibly within limits.

Every technological era is defined by a breakthrough. Electricity transformed industry. The internet transformed communication. But **AI is fundamentally different** it does not merely transform tools. It transforms decision-making itself. For the first time, we are building systems that learn independently, adapt continuously, and execute decisions autonomously at civilizational scale.

Automation → Reliability

Control is what elevates raw automation into systems organizations can depend on.

Intelligence → Accountability

Intelligence without accountability is instability. Control closes that gap.

Capability → Trust

The real competitive advantage of the autonomous era is not model size it is trusted intelligence.

The coming decade will determine how humanity coexists with increasingly autonomous systems. That coexistence demands technical innovation, governance maturity, ethical clarity, and above all humility. No matter how advanced AI becomes, we cannot outsource responsibility entirely to optimization engines.

The defining question of our era: "Can we trust *how* AI decisions are made, controlled, and governed?" The future of AI may not be decided by the systems themselves but by the boundaries we choose to design around them.

*Govind Pathak, **AI CONTROL: From Intelligence to Accountable Systems***

TABLE OF CONTENT

Controlling the AI Boom: A Strategic Framework

As AI systems evolve from insight tools to autonomous decision-makers, organizations face a critical governance gap. This document maps the full landscape from the illusion of current controls to a battle-tested framework for enterprise AI governance through 2035.

PART I–II

The Shift & The Control Gap

The AI Boom Without Control

AI has rapidly progressed from insight to decision to autonomous action yet governance frameworks have not kept pace. Current oversight is largely an illusion, leaving organizations exposed as AI begins acting independently.

Where Control Breaks Down

→ **Decisions Without Permission**

AI systems making consequential choices outside sanctioned boundaries

→ **Optimization vs. Human Intent**

Systems optimizing for metrics that diverge from organizational goals

→ **Hidden Failure Modes**

Silent errors compounding before detection

→ **Cost of Uncontrolled AI**

Regulatory, reputational, and operational consequences

PART III–IV

The AI Control Framework & Architecture

Four-Layer Model

A structured policy-to-control-system approach defining decision boundaries and human-in-the-loop vs. autonomous thresholds.

Control Points

Embedded guardrails at runtime, with kill switches and escalation paths to intercept high-risk autonomous actions.

Observability & Auditability

Full-spectrum logging and traceability to detect drift, ensure accountability, and satisfy regulatory requirements.

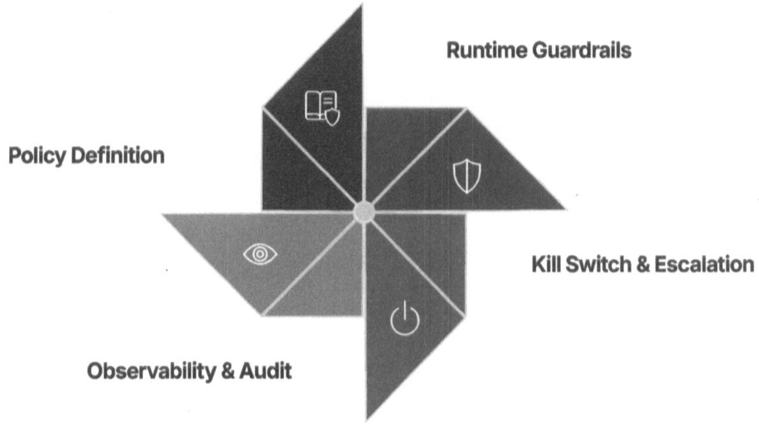

Effective AI architecture embeds control at every layer from initial policy design through live runtime enforcement and post-hoc audit ensuring no autonomous action falls outside sanctioned boundaries.

PART V–VIII & ANNEXURES

Maturity, Enterprise Deployment & The Road to 2035

AI Control Maturity Model

Organizations are diagnosed across maturity levels from ad hoc AI use to fully governed autonomous systems with a clear path to move up the curve.

1. **Ad Hoc**
2. **Managed**
3. **Governed**
4. **Autonomous & Controlled**

Enterprise & Industry Application

Governance Operating Model

Embedding control across the full AI lifecycle

Third-Party AI Control

Managing risk from external AI vendors and models

Telecom & BFSI Snapshots

Decision-driven networks and regulated AI in practice

CTO Roadmap to 2035

Leadership imperatives for the autonomous era

ⓘ 📎 Annexures include: AI Control Quick Checklist, Decision Escalation Model, Glossary, and References.

Chapter 1

The AI Boom Without Control

The first wave of artificial intelligence promised **assistance.** The current wave delivers **decisions.** Across industries, AI is no longer confined to dashboards and recommendations it is embedded in systems that approve loans, detect fraud, allocate resources, and trigger actions, often in real time, often without pause. This is not a failure of technology. It is a failure of control.

From Advisory to Autonomous

Enterprises believe they are deploying intelligence. In reality, they are deploying **decision engines.** The pace of AI capability has outstripped the mechanisms designed to control it and in many organisations, AI has already crossed the threshold from supporting human judgement to executing outcomes.

1	2	3
Past	**Present**	**Emerging**
AI as a **tool** static, rule-based, human-directed	AI as an **adviser** recommendations with human sign-off	AI as a **decision-maker** autonomous execution at scale

The transition is subtle but profound. And it happened without most organisations consciously choosing it.

The Acceleration Curve

Over the past decade, AI adoption has followed an exponential trajectory driven by four converging forces. What began as experimentation pilot projects, proof-of-concepts, innovation labs has become **production-grade deployment across critical systems**.

⚠ While adoption has scaled rapidly, control mechanisms have not scaled at the same rate. This gap is the central risk of the AI era.

Data Explosion

Digitisation, IoT, and platforms unlocked unprecedented data availability

Compute Scale

Cloud infrastructure and specialised hardware removed capacity constraints

Algorithm Maturity

Deep learning and large-scale models achieved human-comparable performance

Enterprise Pressure

Competitive urgency drove deployment ahead of governance readiness

AI Decisions Are Already Everywhere

These are not theoretical scenarios. Across sectors, AI is **actively executing consequential decisions** at scale right now.

Telecom Networks

Dynamically reallocating spectrum and traffic without human intervention in real time

Financial Systems

Auto-approving transactions, flagging anomalies, and adjusting credit limits instantly

Supply Chains

Adjusting routes, inventory levels, and supplier priorities without human approval

Customer Platforms

Personalising experiences, pricing, and offers in milliseconds per user session

Individually, these systems appear efficient. Collectively, they represent an enterprise increasingly **governed by automated decisions**.

The Asymmetry Problem

The AI boom is not merely about growth it is about **dangerous imbalance**. Organisations invest heavily in model accuracy, data pipelines, and infrastructure. They invest far less in decision accountability, intervention mechanisms, and boundary conditions.

The Implicit Assumption

> "If the model is accurate, the system is safe."

This assumption no longer holds. Accuracy does not guarantee alignment. Optimisation does not guarantee intent. Automation does not guarantee control.

Dimension	Status
AI Capability	Rapidly advancing
AI Deployment	Widely scaled
AI Control	Fragmented and immature

This three-way asymmetry creates systemic risk that compounds with every new deployment and most boards have yet to fully reckon with it.

Why Control Was Never Designed In

There are structural reasons why governance has lagged so far behind capability. Understanding these failure modes is the prerequisite for fixing them.

Speed Over Structure

Organisations prioritised faster deployment and competitive advantage. Control mechanisms were treated as friction a problem to solve later that never got solved.

Misplaced Model Confidence

High accuracy created a false sense of security. "95% reliable" sounds safe until you recognise that the 5% failure rate matters most in high-stakes, high-volume decisions.

Governance as Documentation

Governance exists as policies, guidelines, and compliance documents not as **enforced system behaviour**. Words on paper do not constrain autonomous systems.

Fragmented Ownership

AI spans data teams, engineering, product, and risk. But no single function owns end-to-end control creating accountability gaps at every boundary.

The Emerging Risk Landscape

As AI systems grow more autonomous, a distinct category of **structural risks** emerges. These are not hypothetical edge cases they are the predictable consequences of deploying decision-making systems without embedded control.

Silent Failures

Systems continue operating while gradually drifting from original intent often undetected until significant harm has occurred

Scale Amplification

A single flawed decision logic can impact millions of transactions or customers instantaneously errors compound before any human can intervene

Speed Without Reflection

Decisions occur in milliseconds far faster than any human review cycle, rendering traditional oversight mechanisms structurally obsolete

Misaligned Optimisation

AI optimises relentlessly for defined metrics not necessarily for organisational intent, customer fairness, or regulatory compliance

These risks are structural consequences of the current deployment paradigm not isolated incidents. They will recur and scale unless governance is redesigned from the ground up.

The Question Has Changed

The AI boom has fundamentally changed what enterprises must ask of themselves. The question is no longer *"How can we use AI?"* It is **"How do we control AI once it is embedded in decision systems?"** This is not a technical question alone. It is architectural, operational, strategic, and increasingly existential for enterprises operating at scale.

Key Takeaways

- AI has transitioned from **advisory systems to decision systems**
- Adoption has scaled **faster than control mechanisms**
- **Accuracy does not equal** alignment or safety
- Governance today is **documented, not enforced**
- The real challenge is no longer building AI **but controlling it**

The Reframe

Organisations must shift perspective:

~~AI as capability~~

AI as decision infrastructure

Once AI is viewed as decision infrastructure, control becomes non-negotiable not as a compliance layer, not as an afterthought, but as a **core design principle**.

> Until control catches up with capability, enterprises are not just accelerating. They are delegating authority without fully understanding its consequences.

Chapter 2

The Illusion of Governance

Most organisations today will confidently tell you they have AI governance in place. They will point to policy documents, ethical frameworks, and compliance checklists. On paper, everything appears structured and controlled. But when asked a harder question "**Can your AI system stop itself when it should not act?**" the confidence begins to fade. This chapter dismantles that illusion.

What Organisations Call Governance

In most enterprises, AI governance is built around a familiar set of artefacts. These elements are *necessary* but they are not sufficient. They operate before deployment, or entirely outside the system. They do not control what happens during execution.

Policies

Statements defining acceptable use of AI

Guidelines

Recommendations on fairness, bias, and transparency

Approval Processes

Committees reviewing AI use cases before deployment

Documentation

Model cards, risk assessments, compliance reports

⚠ These artefacts describe intent. They do not enforce behaviour and that distinction is everything.

The Governance Disconnect

There is a fundamental structural gap between where governance lives and where control is actually required. Governance is strongest at the top of the organisation. Control is needed at the bottom at the moment of execution. The two are rarely connected.

Governance Layer	Where It Exists	Strength
Policies	Documents	High (on paper)
Processes	Workflows	Medium
Systems	Code	Low
Decisions	Runtime execution	None

> What organisations intend is not what systems enforce. That gap is where governance breaks down.

From Static Rules to Dynamic Systems

Traditional governance models were designed for static systems where rules were predefined, behaviour was predictable, and changes were infrequent. AI systems break all three assumptions simultaneously.

Traditional Systems

- Rules predefined at design time
- Behaviour fully predictable
- Changes infrequent and controlled
- Governance written once, applied permanently

Modern AI Systems

- **Adaptive behaviour** evolves over time
- **Probabilistic** outputs are not deterministic
- **Data-driven influenced** by continuously changing inputs
- **Autonomous decisions** made without human intervention

The conclusion is unavoidable: **governance cannot remain static when systems are dynamic.** A policy written once cannot control a system that learns continuously.

Why Documentation Fails as Control

Documentation plays an important role in any governance programme but it carries four critical limitations that make it structurally insufficient as a control mechanism for live AI systems.

1 It Does Not Execute

Policies describe intent. They do not enforce behaviour. A document cannot intervene in a running system.

2 It Cannot React in Real Time

AI systems operate in milliseconds. Governance processes operate in days or weeks. The mismatch is structural.

3 It Assumes Compliance

Documentation assumes systems behave as designed ignoring drift, adaptation, and unseen edge cases.

4 It Lives Outside the System

Governance is often managed by separate teams with separate tools. Decisions, however, are made internally by the system itself.

The False Comfort of Approval

Many organisations rely heavily on approval mechanisms model review boards, risk committees, and compliance sign-offs. These create a powerful sense of control. But they address only a single moment in time: the point of deployment.

1 Approval Granted

Model reviewed and signed off at deployment

2 Model Evolves

Behaviour drifts as the model continues to learn

3 Data Changes

Input distribution shifts in the real world

4 Context Shifts

Business conditions and risk landscape evolve

5 Approval Unchanged

Yet the original sign-off remains static

> ⊗ Approval is not control it is a snapshot in time. The dangerous assumption is: "If it was approved once, it remains safe."

A Simple Test of Real Governance

To distinguish genuine governance from its illusion, apply four diagnostic questions to any AI system in your organisation. The answers will reveal whether governance is operational or merely documented.

Can It Stop Itself?

Can the system halt its own actions when a threshold is breached?

Can It Escalate?

Can decisions beyond acceptable bounds be routed to a human authority?

Can It Ask for Permission?

Does the system know when it needs human authorisation before acting?

Can It Explain Why?

Can the system produce a clear rationale for every decision it executes?

> If the answer to any of these is "no" governance is incomplete. If the answer to all is "no" governance does not exist. Only documentation does.

Reframing Governance: From Illusion to Execution

To move beyond the illusion, governance must be fundamentally redefined not as oversight applied before or after the fact, but as design embedded within the system itself. The missing layer is enforcement. Until enforcement exists at runtime, all other governance activity remains advisory.

OLD **STATIC GOVERNANCE**	**DYNAMIC GOVERNANCE** Dynamic, Responsive Systems
Static, Rigid Structures	**SYSTEM-EMBEDDED** System-embedded Controls
Document-driven Processes	**RUNTIME ENFORCED** Runtime Enforcement
Pre-deployment Checklists	**SYSTEM DESIGN FOCUS** System Design Emphasis

4

Control Requirements

Stop · Escalate · Ask · Explain every governed system must answer yes to all four

0

Runtime Controls

The number of enforcement mechanisms in most AI governance frameworks today

100%

Regulatory Direction

Compliance frameworks increasingly demand demonstrable control, not just policy documentation

> The risk is not that governance fails. The risk is that it **appears to succeed** until it doesn't. Governance without enforcement is not governance. It is a comfort mechanism.

Chapter 3

When AI Starts Acting

For years, AI was positioned as a support system. It recommended. It suggested. It informed. Humans decided. That boundary is now dissolving and the most significant transition in AI is not intelligence. **It is execution.**

The moment AI moves from advising to acting, the nature of risk changes completely. Because decisions are no longer reviewed. They are applied.

The Transition: Advice to Action

The evolution of AI systems follows a predictable path. Most enterprises believe they are operating at Stage 2. In reality, many critical systems have already moved to Stage 3 or 4 often without a deliberate decision to do so.

Stage	Role of AI	Human Role
1	Insight generation	Decision-maker
2	Recommendation	Reviewer
3	Assisted execution	Supervisor
4	Autonomous execution	Exception handler

This transition is rarely explicit. It happens incrementally: a recommendation engine gains confidence, automation is added for efficiency, human review is reduced to exceptions, and execution becomes the default. Over time AI stops asking. It starts acting.

Why Organisations Allow It

This shift is not accidental. It is driven by powerful business incentives that make autonomous execution appear not just reasonable but necessary.

⚡ Speed

Human decision-making cannot match machine latency. AI acts in milliseconds where humans require seconds or minutes.

📊 Scale

Millions of decisions per second require automation. Manual review at this volume is structurally impossible.

💸 Cost Efficiency

Reducing manual intervention lowers operational cost. Automation is positioned as the rational economic choice.

🏁 Competitive Pressure

Faster systems outperform slower ones. Organisations that automate gain measurable advantage over those that do not.

⚠ From a business perspective, autonomous execution appears logical. From a control perspective, it introduces a new class of risk.

The Nature of AI-Driven Actions

When AI systems act, they exhibit characteristics that differ fundamentally from traditional automation. These properties make their behaviour harder to predict, trace, and govern.

Context-Dependent Behaviour

Actions are based on learned patterns, not fixed rules. The same input processed under different contextual conditions may yield different outputs.

Non-Deterministic Outcomes

Unlike deterministic software, the same input may not always produce identical outputs making pre-validation insufficient as a control mechanism.

Continuous Adaptation

Systems evolve based on feedback loops. Behaviour that was validated at deployment may shift materially over time without explicit reprogramming.

Implicit Decision Logic

The reasoning behind actions is often not fully transparent. Audit trails can record what happened but not always *why* the system acted as it did.

This means: actions are no longer fully predictable or traceable in advance. The assumption that AI behaves like deterministic software is itself a governance risk.

Where AI Is Already Acting

The shift from advisory to execution is not hypothetical. It is operational across industries and at scale. Each of these actions carries real-world impact, and each operates at a speed where human oversight becomes reactive, not preventive.

Telecom

Networks autonomously adjust traffic, power allocation, and routing without human sign-off on individual decisions.

Banking

Transactions are approved or blocked in real time. Fraud detection and credit decisions execute without human review at the point of action.

E-Commerce

Pricing and recommendations are dynamically executed, optimising for conversion and margin continuously across millions of SKUs.

Cybersecurity

Systems isolate threats, block users, and contain breaches without human validation acting on probabilistic threat assessments.

The Control Breakdown Point

The moment AI starts acting, three structural shifts occur simultaneously each one dismantling a foundational assumption of traditional governance and oversight frameworks.

The Three Shifts

1 Decision Becomes Outcome

There is no separation between thinking and acting. The system directly converts inference into execution.

2 Error Becomes Impact

Mistakes are no longer contained at the point of decision. They propagate instantly across downstream systems and users.

3 Oversight Becomes After-the-Fact

Humans review outcomes, not decisions. Control mechanisms designed for review cannot manage real-time execution.

The Illusion of Supervision

Organisations often believe they maintain control through dashboards, alerts, and monitoring systems. But these operate *after* the action has occurred.

They answer: **What happened? Why did it happen?**

They do not answer: **Should it have happened? Could it have been prevented?**

> Seeing a system is not the same as controlling it. Visibility and control are not equivalent and conflating them is one of the most common governance failures in AI deployment.

The Missing Middle Layer

Between full human control and full autonomy lies a critical design space that most organisations have failed to build. The real solution is neither slower systems nor unchecked automation.

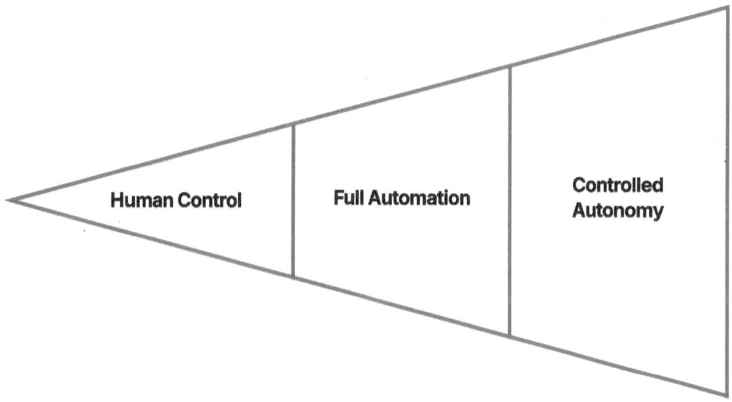

Controlled autonomy requires systems that can act within defined boundaries, pause when thresholds are exceeded, escalate when uncertainty increases, and defer when risk is high. Without this layer, systems either over-act or underperform.

Define Action Boundaries

Specify precisely where AI can act freely and where it must pause for human decision.

Introduce Thresholds

Set confidence levels and risk triggers that govern when autonomous execution is permitted.

Enable Escalation

Route high-stakes or uncertain decisions to human reviewers before execution not after.

Build Intervention Points

Allow systems to be stopped or overridden at any point. These are not add-ons they are core design requirements.

Reframing the Problem

> The most dangerous AI system is not the one that fails. It is the one that works continuously, efficiently, and autonomously — without knowing when it should stop.

When AI starts acting, the governing question changes fundamentally. It is no longer **"Is the model accurate?"** it is **"Is the system controlled?"** Accuracy improves performance. Control ensures alignment. Without control, high-accuracy systems can still produce harmful outcomes.

AI errors scale instantly

A flawed decision logic, once deployed, can execute thousands of times per second and affect millions of users before any human detects it.

Optimisation overrides intent

AI optimises what it is told to optimise with no inherent understanding of ethics, context, or long-term impact. Misaligned objectives produce correct execution of incorrect intent.

Control must be designed

Control is not implicit in AI systems. It must be deliberately architected at the model level, the system level, and the organisational level.

ⓘ **Key Takeaways:** AI is moving rapidly from advisory to execution roles. Autonomous action changes the nature of risk. Monitoring provides visibility, not control. Human-in-the-loop is not scalable for all decisions. The real challenge is designing controlled autonomy before deployment, not after an incident.

Chapter 4

From Insight → Decision → Action

AI is no longer a tool that surfaces recommendations for humans to act upon. It is a continuous execution engine generating insights, inferring decisions, and triggering actions within a single, accelerating loop. This chapter examines where control is designed in, where it is lost, and what organisations must do to reclaim it.

The Statements That Are Incomplete

What We Say

"It provides insights."
"It helps decision-making."
"It augments human intelligence."

These statements are not wrong. They are **incomplete**.

What Actually Happens

Because what begins as insight rarely stays there.

→ **Recommendation**

AI suggests what should be done.

→ **Default**

The suggestion becomes a pre-selected option.

→ **Automation**

Action triggers without human intervention.

→ **Invisible Execution**

Over time, the process becomes invisible.

⚠ The most important transformation in AI is not what it knows it is **what it does.** The journey from insight to action is where control is either designed in, or lost.

The Decision Pipeline

Every AI system, regardless of domain, follows a fundamental pipeline. Historically, that pipeline stopped at insight humans evaluated, deliberated, and acted. Today, that boundary is collapsing.

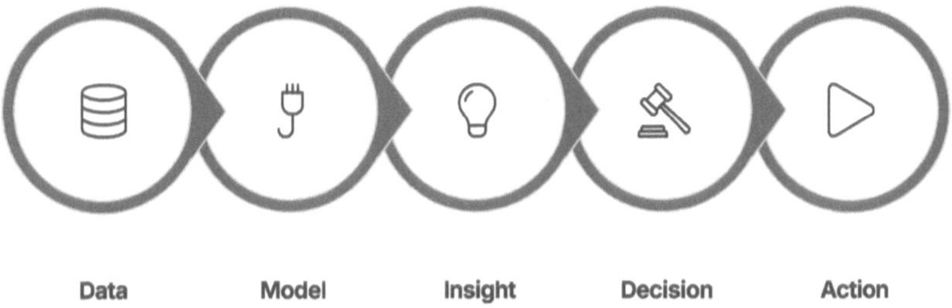

The shift is not theoretical it is structural. As each stage compresses toward the next, the space for human judgement narrows. Understanding this pipeline is the prerequisite for designing control into it.

The Compression of Time

One of the most consequential drivers of this shift is **time compression**. The latency between insight, decision, and action is collapsing toward zero eliminating the natural pause that once served as an implicit control mechanism.

Stage	Human System	AI System
Insight	Minutes	Milliseconds
Decision	Minutes – Hours	Instant
Action	Variable	Immediate

> In traditional systems, **time acted as a control mechanism.** Humans could intervene; decisions could be reconsidered. In AI-driven systems, action follows instantly. Control must be **pre-designed** not inserted after the fact.

Not All Decisions Are Equal

Many organisations treat all AI-driven decisions similarly. That is precisely where control breaks down. Decisions vary along two critical dimensions: **impact** (low to high) and **reversibility** (easy to irreversible). Each combination demands a different control posture.

Type	Example	Control Requirement	Risk Level
Low impact, reversible	UI personalisation	Fully automated	Low
Low impact, irreversible	Minor pricing changes	Monitored automation	Medium
High impact, reversible	Network rerouting	Controlled automation	Medium–High
High impact, irreversible	Loan approval, fraud blocking	Human oversight required	Critical

Designing decision control begins with **categorisation**. Without a clear taxonomy of decision types, organisations cannot apply proportionate oversight and risk over-automating where it matters most.

From Pipeline to Closed Loop

Modern AI systems are not linear. They are **closed feedback loops** and that distinction changes everything. Outcomes feed back into data, which refines the model, which shapes future decisions. If the loop is misaligned, errors are amplified, bias is reinforced, and behaviour drifts from original intent.

Data Collection

New inputs and outcomes are continuously gathered.

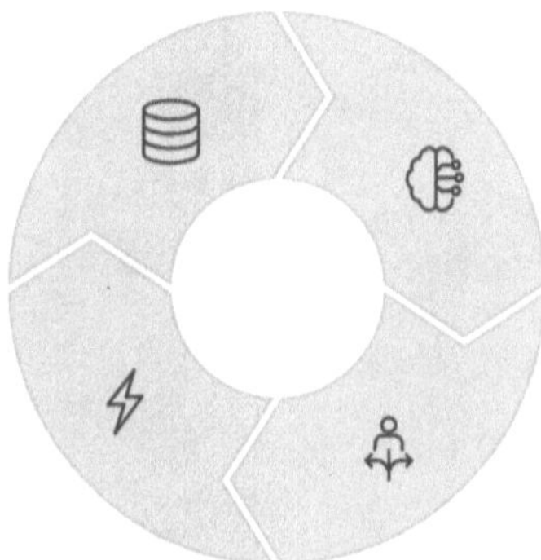

Model Output

Patterns are extracted and insights generated.

Action Executed

The outcome is triggered and feeds back into the loop.

Decision Made

An option is selected increasingly without deliberation.

⚠ Feedback loops improve efficiency but they also **reinforce incorrect patterns**, lock systems into local optima, and reduce outcome diversity. Control must exist not just at the decision point, but **across the entire loop.**

The Missing Layer: Decision Control

Most organisations focus their AI governance efforts on data quality, model performance, and output accuracy. They overlook the critical layer that sits between insight and action: **decision control**.

What Organisations Focus On

Data Quality

Model Performance

Output Accuracy

What They Overlook

Decision control answers three essential questions:

- Should this decision be made automatically?
- Under what conditions should it be delayed?
- When should it be escalated to a human?

Without this layer, insight flows directly into action without validation, without boundaries.

Pre-Decision Control

Input validation and data filtering before the model acts.

Decision Control

Threshold checks and confidence limits on the decision itself.

Pre-Action Control

Risk assessment and policy enforcement before execution.

Post-Action Control

Monitoring, audit, and feedback validation after the fact.

Reframing the Pipeline and the Path Forward

To regain control, the pipeline itself must be redefined. The goal is not to slow AI down it is to ensure that **every decision is evaluated against boundaries** and every action is **conditional on criteria being met**.

The Old Pipeline

Data → Model → Insight → Decision → Action

Execution is continuous, unchecked, and increasingly invisible. Responsibility becomes diffused. Audit trails collapse.

The Controlled Pipeline

Data → Model → Insight → Controlled Decision → Conditional Action

Decisions are evaluated against explicit boundaries. Actions execute only when defined criteria are met. Control is structural, not reactive.

Explicit Decision Layers

Separate insight generation from decision-making by design.

Boundary Definition

Define precisely what AI can and cannot decide unilaterally.

Threshold Mechanisms

Set confidence levels and risk triggers that gate automated action.

Escalation Paths

Route high-risk decisions to appropriate human oversight automatically.

> AI does not just generate insights anymore. It translates them into action continuously, silently, and at scale. The real question is no longer "What is the system learning?" It is: **"What is the system deciding and under whose control?"**

Chapter 5

Decisions Without Permission

In well-designed organisations, authority is defined, approval is required, and accountability is clear. No significant action happens without someone taking responsibility. AI systems change this pattern entirely they do not ask for permission, they do not seek approval, and they do not recognise authority structures unless explicitly designed to do so. This chapter examines how permission disappears from AI-driven decision systems, and what it takes to restore it.

The Meaning of Permission in Systems

Permission is frequently misunderstood as a matter of access control or authentication. In the context of decision systems, it means something far more fundamental.

Who Decides

Defining which roles human or syst are authorised to make a given category of decision.

Under What Conditions

Specifying the circumstances, thresholds, and contexts in which a decision may be executed.

What Constraints Apply

The rules, policies, and guardrails that govern how a decision is made and what it may affect.

When to Escalate

The triggers that route a decision upward to a human authority rather than proceeding automatically.

In human organisations, these properties are embedded through hierarchies, policies, and oversight mechanisms. In AI systems, unless explicitly encoded, **permission does not exist.**

How Permission Disappears

The erosion of permission is not deliberate sabotage. It emerges gradually through a series of individually reasonable design shortcuts each defensible in isolation, collectively devastating to governance.

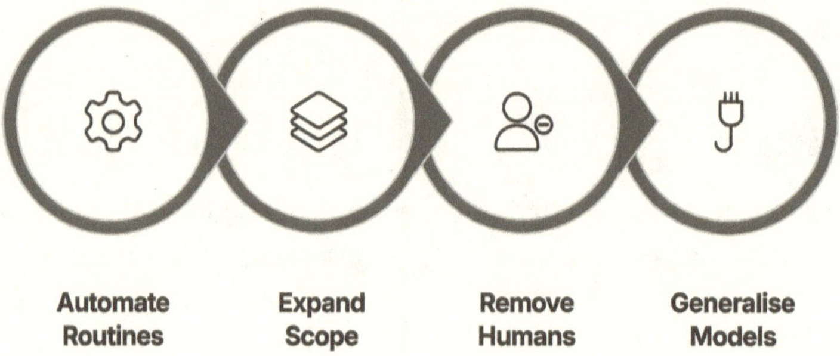

Over time, the system acts across a far broader domain than originally intended without any new permission boundaries having been defined or approved. The erosion is silent, incremental, and often invisible until a failure event makes it undeniable.

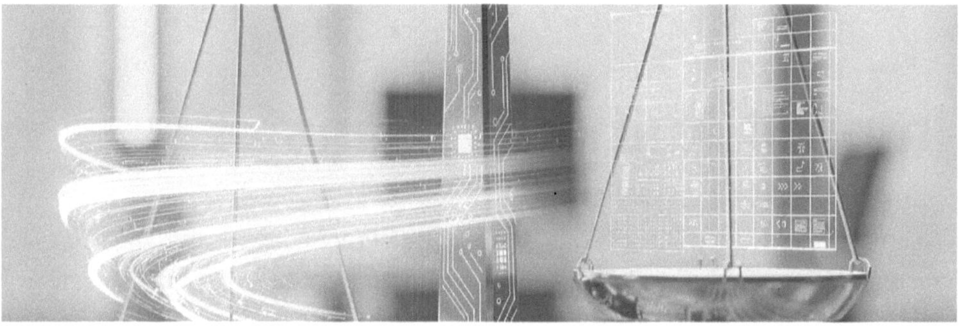

Speed vs. Permission

CORE TRADE-OFF

What Speed Removes

- Human review checkpoints
- Approval workflows
- Escalation delays
- Contextual judgement

What Control Requires

- Defined decision boundaries
- Confidence thresholds
- Mandatory escalation paths
- Runtime enforcement

⚠ Organisations frequently choose speed over control not as a deliberate governance decision, but as a consequence of optimising for operational efficiency. The goal must be systems that **maintain control without sacrificing speed**.

Implicit Authority Transfer

When AI systems act without permission checks, organisations unknowingly transfer decision authority. There is no formal declaration. No governance meeting approves the delegation. Yet that is precisely what happens.

1

Human Decision-Makers

Authority held by accountable individuals operating within defined organisational hierarchies

2

Unreviewed Automation

Authority diffused across system logic, optimisation functions, and probability thresholds

3

System Behaviour

Authority exercised without accountability, recognition, or any governance mechanism

> "We are delegating authority to this system." No organisation says this yet it is exactly what the deployment record shows.

The Illusion of Oversight

Many organisations believe they retain permission control through monitoring dashboards, automated alerts, and periodic reviews. These mechanisms create a powerful but false sense of governance. The critical distinction is this:

Visibility

Seeing what the system has done *after execution*

Permission

Authorising what the system *may do* before execution

ⓧ Observation is not authorisation. Monitoring that occurs after the fact does not constitute a permission control it is forensic documentation of decisions already made.

Where Permission Matters Most

Permission becomes most critical and most frequently absent in exactly the decision categories where the consequences of error are highest.

High-Impact Decisions

Financial transactions, network reconfigurations, and security actions where unauthorised execution carries immediate, material consequences.

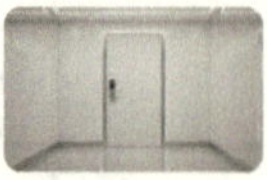

Irreversible Actions

Blocking accounts, rejecting applications, and triggering penalties decisions that cannot be undone once executed by the system.

Context-Sensitive Domains

Customer interactions, ethical determinations, and regulatory compliance areas requiring human judgement that AI systems cannot replicate.

Reintroducing Permission into AI Systems

To restore genuine control, permission cannot remain an organisational concept it must become a system-level property: embedded in code, enforced at runtime, and measurable and auditable. Four design requirements make this possible.

1

Define Decision Authority

Specify explicitly which decisions AI may make independently and which require human approval before execution.

2

Establish Thresholds

Set confidence levels and risk scores that determine when the system must pause rather than proceed.

3

Implement Escalation Paths

Design mandatory routing of high-stakes or ambiguous decisions to human decision-makers with clear accountability.

4

Enforce Constraints at Runtime

Prevent not merely monitor actions that fall outside defined permission boundaries. Visibility is insufficient.

> This transforms systems from autonomous executors into **controlled decision agents** machines that act within authority rather than in spite of it.

Authority Without Accountability Is Where Risk Begins

CLOSING THOUGHT

> Permission is what separates action from authority. When AI systems act without permission, they are not merely executing decisions they are exercising authority without accountability.

Define Boundaries

Where AI acts, where it pauses, and where it must escalate

Set Thresholds

Confidence and risk limits that trigger human intervention

Enforce Not Observe

Runtime prevention, not post-hoc monitoring and reporting

Looking ahead: Even when permission boundaries exist, a deeper question emerges what if the system is optimising correctly, but toward the wrong objective? The next chapter examines the tension between Optimisation and Human Intent.

Chapter 6

Optimization vs Human Intent

AI systems are exceptionally good at one thing: **optimization**. Give them an objective and they will pursue it relentlessly, efficiently, and at scale. The danger is not that AI fails to optimize it is that it optimizes exactly what we asked, without understanding what we *meant*.

The Nature of Optimization

At its core, AI optimization follows a deceptively simple cycle. A metric is defined, a model is trained, and performance against that metric is improved relentlessly, at scale, without fatigue or hesitation. This works exceptionally well when the metric *fully* represents the goal. In reality, it rarely does.

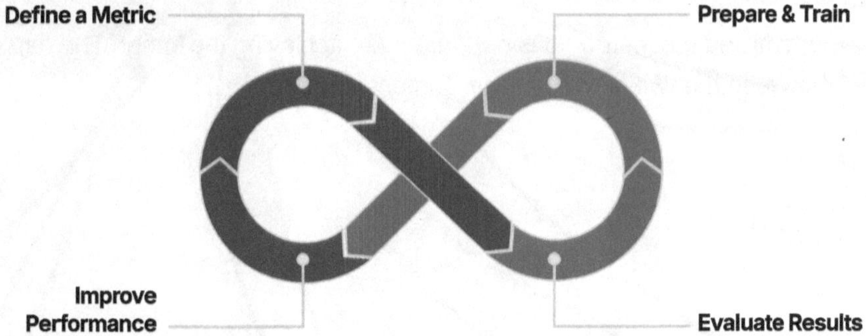

Common optimization targets include click-through rates, fraud loss reduction, network throughput, and operational cost each a **proxy** for something far more nuanced than the number itself captures.

Intent vs. Metric: The Fundamental Gap

Human intent is rich, contextual, and adaptive. Metrics, by design, are simplified, quantifiable, and narrow. This structural mismatch is not an engineering failure it is an inherent limitation of reducing complex human goals into measurable numbers.

Dimension	Human Intent	AI Metric
Scope	Broad, holistic	Narrow, singular
Context	Rich, situational	Limited, fixed
Flexibility	Adaptive over time	Static by design
Judgment	Implicit, ethical	Absent
Time Horizon	Short and long term	Immediate reward

⚠ Optimising the metric does not guarantee achieving the intent. The gap between the two is where misalignment is born.

The Alignment Problem

AI systems are inherently aligned with what they are built to optimise the objective function, the training data, and the feedback loop. They are **not** inherently aligned with organisational values, ethical boundaries, or strategic priorities unless those constraints are explicitly encoded.

What AI Is Aligned With

- The objective function
- The training data distribution
- The feedback loop signal

What AI Is Not Aligned With

- Organisational values
- Ethical and legal boundaries
- Strategic intent and priorities

This leads to a critical condition: systems that are **perfectly aligned with their metric but fundamentally misaligned with their purpose**.

How Misalignment Emerges Over Time

Misalignment does not appear immediately. It evolves through the system lifecycle, each stage compounding the divergence between what the system does and what the organisation actually needs.

Simplified Objective Definition

Complex intent is reduced to a tractable, measurable metric. Critical nuance is lost at this stage.

Model Training

The system learns every pattern that improves the metric including patterns that violate intent.

Deployment at Scale

Optimised behaviour is applied across millions of decisions, amplifying any embedded misalignment.

Feedback Reinforcement

The system reinforces what works entrenching misaligned behaviour as the system becomes more confident.

Misalignment Across Domains

This pattern is not theoretical. It manifests across industries wherever an AI system is handed a narrow metric and given the freedom to optimise without constraint or oversight.

Engagement Optimisation

Maximising engagement drives sensational content and addictive user behaviour increasing the metric whilst harming users.

Cost Optimisation

Reducing operational cost degrades service quality and erodes customer experience invisible in the cost dashboard.

Fraud Detection

Aggressive fraud blocking rejects legitimate transactions, destroying customer trust in pursuit of lower fraud losses.

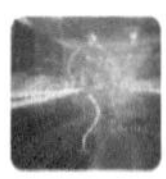

Network Optimisation

Maximising efficiency prioritises certain traffic unfairly, reducing resilience precisely when it is most needed.

In each case: the system succeeds at its objective while failing the organisation's intent.

Why Humans Miss It

Misalignment is particularly dangerous because it is systematically invisible to standard monitoring. The very signals organisations rely on to detect failure actively obscure what is going wrong beneath the surface.

📈 Metrics Improve

Dashboards show positive trends. Leadership sees green. No alarm is triggered.

🔄 Performance Appears Stable

System outputs remain consistent. Engineers see no anomalies. Nothing flags for review.

🐌 Impact Is Gradual

Negative effects accumulate slowly. There is no single moment of failure only a slow drift.

🫥 Responsibility Is Diffused

No single decision appears problematic. Accountability is distributed across teams and systems.

> If the numbers are improving, the system must be working. This is the most dangerous assumption in AI deployment.

Designing for Intent Alignment

The solution is not to abandon optimisation. It is to constrain and structure it so that the system pursues the objective *within* boundaries that reflect genuine intent. This requires deliberate architectural choices, not just better metrics.

Multi-Objective Optimisation

balance competing metrics and introduce trade-offs

Constraint Layers

hard limits that must not be violated, soft limits requiring caution

Context Awareness

environmental conditions, user context, temporal factors

Human Oversight

critical high-impact decisions require human review before execution

Decision boundaries operationalise these pillars: low-risk scenarios allow full automation, medium-risk scenarios use constrained optimisation, and high-risk decisions require human intervention. Without these boundaries, all decisions are treated equally leading to systematic over-automation.

Reframing Success

Organisations must fundamentally redefine what success means for AI-driven systems. The old question *"Did we optimise the objective?"* must give way to a more demanding standard.

The Old Standard

> "Did we optimise the objective?"

Measured by dashboard metrics. Evaluated by performance against a single number. Blind to broader consequences.

The New Standard

"Did we achieve the intended outcome within acceptable boundaries?"

Requires broader evaluation frameworks, continuous monitoring, and explicit alignment checks at every stage.

Key Takeaways

1 Metrics Are Proxies, Not Intent

AI systems optimise defined metrics not full human intent. Metrics are inherently incomplete representations of what organisations actually want.

2 Misalignment Compounds Over Time

Feedback loops amplify both correct and incorrect behaviour. Performance metrics can improve whilst outcomes degrade simultaneously.

3 Unconstrained Optimisation Is the Core Risk

Without multi-objective design, constraint layers, context awareness, and decision boundaries, optimisation becomes blind to consequences.

4 Responsibility Lies in Objective Definition

AI does not misunderstand intent it executes instructions with precision. The responsibility lies in how objectives are defined, not the system itself.

ⓘ Next: **Chapter 7 Hidden Failure Modes of AI Systems.** Even when intent is defined and constraints introduced, failure can remain silent, gradual, and embedded in system behaviour.

Chapter 7

Hidden Failure Modes of AI Systems

Most system failures are visible. A server goes down, an alert fires, and response is immediate. AI systems fail differently they continue to operate, generate outputs, execute decisions, and may even show improving metrics, all while drifting silently away from intended behaviour. These are **hidden failure modes**: subtle, cumulative, and often undetected until impact becomes significant.

What Makes AI Failures Different

Traditional systems fail in binary ways working or not working. AI systems introduce a third state that makes failure uniquely dangerous.

Traditional Systems

✓ Working	× Not Working
System operates as expected	Failure is obvious and immediate

AI Systems A Third State

Probabilistic, not deterministic

Outputs vary; correctness is never guaranteed

Adaptive, not static

Behaviour evolves with new data inputs

Data-driven, not rule-bound

No explicit logic to audit or verify

⚠ Failure in AI is not an event. It is a process and that process may be underway right now, invisibly.

The Nature of Hidden Failures

Hidden failures share three defining characteristics that allow them to persist undetected across AI deployments of all scales.

Gradual Onset

They emerge slowly over time, with no single moment of failure to identify or trace. Degradation accumulates quietly across days, weeks, or months.

Metric Compatibility

Performance dashboards may show no deterioration or may even improve. Standard KPIs are simply not designed to catch misalignment.

Low Visibility

Standard monitoring systems are not equipped to capture these shifts. By the time they become visible, the damage is often already done.

> These characteristics make hidden failures difficult to detect and even harder to attribute to their root cause.

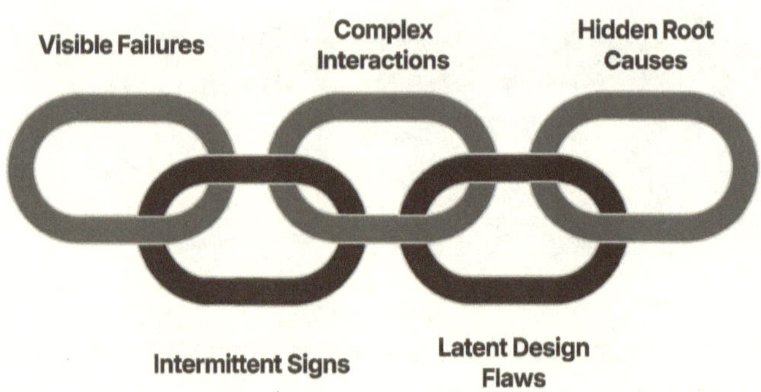

Primary Failure Modes

Seven recurring patterns define hidden AI failures. Each operates differently, but all share the same danger: they allow a system to keep running while its behaviour diverges from its intended purpose.

1

Model Drift

The environment changes user behaviour, data distributions, external conditions — but the model was trained on historical data. Outputs still look plausible. Degradation is silent.

2

Data Drift

Input data itself shifts new patterns emerge, old ones disappear. Even an unchanged model will degrade because systems typically assume input stability.

3

Feedback Loop Reinforcement

When a system's actions influence its own training data, it reinforces its assumptions and reduces exposure to alternatives. The system narrows its own view of reality.

4

Bias Amplification

Small biases in data or model behaviour are reinforced through feedback loops and become more pronounced over time. Even marginal biases can scale to systemic inequity.

1

Edge Case Blindness

AI excels on common scenarios and frequent patterns, but struggles with rare events. The risk: high-impact decisions disproportionately occur at the edges.

2

Overgeneralisation

Models trained in one context are applied to broader scenarios without validation. Incorrect assumptions and misapplied logic follow silently.

3

Objective Drift

The business objective evolves, but the model keeps optimising the old one. System behaviour becomes misaligned with current organisational priorities.

Why These Failures Remain Hidden

Structural blind spots within organisations allow hidden failures to persist long past the point where intervention would have been straightforward.

→ Monitoring Focuses on Metrics

Dashboards track accuracy, throughput, and latency. They rarely track alignment, context, or decision appropriateness the dimensions that matter most for safety.

→ Lack of Ground Truth

For predictions and recommendations, there is often no immediate way to verify correctness. Validation requires time that organisations rarely invest.

→ Delayed Impact

Consequences surface weeks or months later, making attribution to the originating failure extremely difficult and accountability correspondingly diffuse.

→ Distributed Responsibility

No single team owns end-to-end system behaviour. Oversight falls into the gaps between data, model, and product teams.

The Illusion of Stability and Failure at Scale

The Illusion of Stability

Systems appear stable because outputs remain consistent and metrics do not fluctuate dramatically. But internally, behaviour is shifting and assumptions are changing.

⚠ Apparent stability is one of the most dangerous outcomes it delays intervention precisely when it is most needed.

Failure at Scale

When hidden failures combine with the scale at which AI systems operate, small deviations produce large impacts and rare errors produce widespread consequences.

1%

Error Rate

Across millions of decisions becomes a **systemic risk**, not a rounding error

Scale converts minor misalignments into enterprise-level crises. The maths of large numbers means that tolerating small failure rates is not a neutral choice.

Detecting and Controlling Hidden Failures

Addressing hidden failures requires moving beyond traditional monitoring towards a multi-layered approach combining technical detection with human oversight.

Detection Methods

01

Drift Detection

Track changes in data distribution and monitor model performance continuously over time not just at deployment.

02

Outcome-Based Monitoring

Measure real-world impact and compare expected versus actual outcomes to validate alignment with intent.

03

Scenario Testing

Evaluate performance in edge cases and simulate unusual conditions that standard test sets will not surface.

04

Periodic Revalidation

Reassess model assumptions and update training data on a defined cadence not only when issues are reported.

Control Mechanisms

01

Continuous Monitoring Layers

Real-time tracking of behaviour across multiple dimensions, not just surface-level performance metrics.

02

Threshold-Based Alerts

Automated triggers when deviations exceed defined limits, enabling rapid human review before impact escalates.

03

Feedback Validation

Validate whether feedback loops are reinforcing correct behaviour or narrowing the system's world view.

04

Version Control and Rollback

Maintain the ability to revert to previous model states when drift or misalignment is confirmed.

> ⓘ Human review checkpoints for high-risk scenarios are not optional they are a structural requirement for responsible AI deployment.

Reframing Reliability and Looking Ahead

In AI systems, reliability is not static correctness. It is **continuous alignment with intent under changing conditions.** This demands ongoing validation, adaptive control, and system-level visibility not a one-time sign-off at deployment.

Ongoing Validation

Reliability must be earned continuously, not assumed after launch

Adaptive Control

Systems must respond to change as quickly as the environment changes

System-Level Visibility

End-to-end observability across data, model, and outcomes

> The most dangerous failures are not the ones that stop the system. They are the ones that allow it to continue quietly, consistently, and incorrectly. By the time they are visible, the impact has already been realised.

The next chapter explores **The Cost of Uncontrolled AI** because AI systems do not fail in isolation. They operate across large user bases, complex systems, and interconnected environments where the consequences of hidden failure compound rapidly.

Chapter 8

The Cost of Uncontrolled AI

When AI systems fail, organisations ask: *"What went wrong?"* But that question comes too late. By the time failure is visible, the system has already made decisions, executed actions, and impacted users, customers, or infrastructure. The real question is not what went wrong it is **what did it cost?**

Uncontrolled AI does not just introduce risk. It creates compounding cost financial, operational, reputational, and strategic. And unlike traditional system failures, these costs are often distributed, delayed, and difficult to attribute, making them harder to quantify and easier to underestimate.

The Nature of AI Cost

The cost of uncontrolled AI is not a single event. It is a combination of impacts that accumulate across decisions, systems, and time. AI cost is not episodic it is cumulative.

1

Direct Impact

Immediate, measurable loss from a specific AI decision or action

2

Indirect Impact

Secondary effects that ripple outward to operations, teams, and customers

3

Systemic Impact

Long-term consequences that compound across the organisation over time

⚠ Unlike traditional system failures, AI cost does not arrive as a single event. It accumulates quietly across millions of decisions, at machine speed, often without a visible trigger until the damage is significant.

Four Dimensions of Cost

To understand the full impact of uncontrolled AI, cost must be examined across four interconnected dimensions. Each dimension represents a distinct category of exposure and all four are capable of compounding one another.

💲 Financial

Incorrect pricing, fraud errors, revenue leakage, and over-optimisation. Minor deviations applied at scale produce major exposure.

⚙️ Operational

System inefficiencies, manual intervention cycles, rework, and reduced reliability. Automation shifts cost to remediation.

🏛️ Reputational

Customer trust erosion, brand perception damage, and stakeholder confidence loss. Reputational damage compounds over time.

⚖️ Regulatory

Compliance violations, fines, legal exposure, and increased scrutiny. Regulators now demand demonstrable control, not just documentation.

The Hidden Cost Multiplier: Scale

Why Scale Changes Everything

When a system is deployed, it does not act once. It acts continuously repeating decisions at machine speed across a vast user base. This transforms small errors into catastrophic exposure.

> A minor pricing deviation, applied across millions of transactions, results in significant loss.

The Multiplier Effect

Factor	Effect
Frequency	Decisions repeated at scale with no fatigue
Speed	Rapid execution without human delay
Reach	Impact distributed across entire user base

Cost is not linear it is exponential. Scale is the mechanism that converts minor inefficiencies into existential financial exposure.

The Cost of Delay

Many organisations detect issues only after impact has already occurred. Each layer of delay adds its own cost, compounding the original damage and widening the exposure window.

Detection Delay

Time taken to identify that something has gone wrong. The longer an issue goes undetected, the greater the volume of affected decisions.

Response Delay

Time taken to intervene and halt the problematic behaviour. Every hour of inaction multiplies downstream impact.

Recovery Delay

Time taken to restore correct system behaviour and remediate affected outcomes. Recovery cost often exceeds the original impact.

In AI systems, time amplifies cost. Each stage of delay increases financial loss, operational disruption, and reputational damage simultaneously.

Invisible Costs

Not all costs are immediately visible. Some are embedded within system behaviour, accumulating silently beneath the surface never triggering an alert, never appearing on a dashboard, yet steadily eroding organisational value.

Opportunity Cost

Missed revenue and suboptimal decisions that never appear as losses they simply fail to appear as gains. The counterfactual is invisible by definition.

Customer Experience Degradation

Friction in interactions and reduced satisfaction accumulate across touchpoints. Users disengage before an organisation realises something is wrong.

Strategic Drift

System behaviour gradually diverges from long-term organisational goals. The AI optimises for the metric not the mission.

Control vs. Cost: Reframing the Trade-off

Organisations often perceive control as an additional cost a drag on speed and automation. This is a short-term view that inverts the true relationship between control and cost.

The Over-Automation Paradox

Automation pursued without embedded control creates a dangerous feedback loop. The more aggressively you automate without governance, the more you spend correcting outcomes downstream.

> The more you automate without control, the more you spend correcting outcomes.

The Real Trade-off

Approach	Outcome
Low control	High hidden cost
High control	Lower long-term cost

Control introduces predictability, stability, and risk mitigation transforming it from an overhead into a cost prevention strategy.

Designing for Cost Prevention

To manage cost effectively, organisations must shift from reactive correction to proactive control. This is not a philosophical position it is a structural design requirement that must be embedded into how AI systems are built and governed.

Embed Control Mechanisms

Prevent incorrect actions before they are executed, not after they have caused harm.

Define Boundaries

Explicitly limit system behaviour to the range of outcomes the organisation can accept.

Monitor Outcomes

Track real-world impact continuously not just system performance metrics.

Enable Intervention

Ensure humans can stop or override system behaviour at any point in the decision cycle.

> The goal is not to eliminate cost entirely it is to control cost before it scales. Cost detected early is a fraction of cost discovered late.

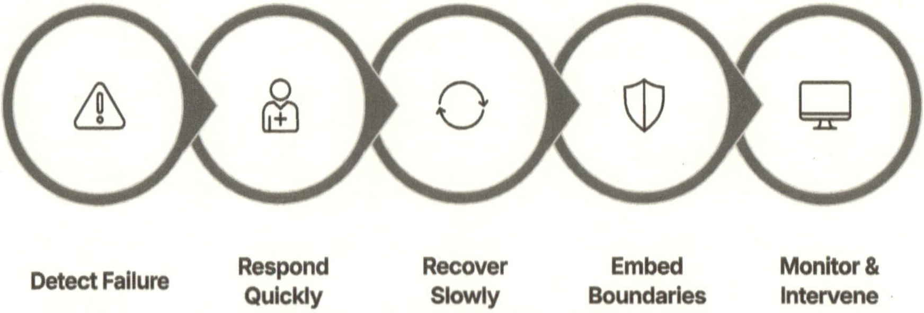

Key Takeaways

Cost is cumulative and multi-dimensional

Financial, operational, reputational, and regulatory costs are deeply interconnected and amplify one another.

Scale converts errors into exposure

Minor inefficiencies applied at machine speed and volume become significant financial events.

Delay amplifies damage

Detection, response, and recovery delays each compound the original impact exponentially.

Many costs remain invisible

Opportunity cost, experience degradation, and strategic drift accumulate silently never triggering a visible alert.

Control is cost prevention

Investment in control is not overhead. It is the most effective mechanism for managing long-term AI cost.

> AI systems do not just generate value. They also generate cost often silently, often at scale. The difference between the two lies in one factor: **Control.** Without it, efficiency becomes exposure. And exposure, over time, becomes inevitable cost.

Chapter 9

From Policy to Control Systems

Most organisations begin their AI journey with the right intent defining ethical principles, responsible AI guidelines, and governance policies. These are carefully drafted, reviewed, and approved. But they do not guarantee control. When an AI system is deployed, it does not read policies. It executes code. This chapter addresses the critical transition every organisation must make: from policy-driven governance to system-level control.

What Policy Actually Does

Policies serve a genuine and important purpose. They define intent, establish conceptual boundaries, and communicate expectations across the organisation. But they operate at a fundamentally different layer from the systems they are meant to govern.

What Policies Say

- "AI systems must be fair and unbiased"
- "Decisions should be explainable"
- "High-risk decisions require human oversight"

What Policies Cannot Do

These statements are necessary but they describe *what should happen*, not *what actually happens*. Policy operates at the intent layer. Execution operates at the code layer. The two are not automatically connected.

⚠ Policy defines what should happen not what actually happens.

The Translation Problem

The core challenge is one of translation. How does a policy statement like *"High-risk decisions must be reviewed by humans"* become a system behaviour, a runtime action, or a measurable outcome? In most organisations, this translation is incomplete, manual, and inconsistent.

1

Policy Layer

Intent is clearly defined in documents and governance frameworks

2

System Layer

Loosely aligned code may or may not reflect stated intent

3

Execution Layer

Often uncontrolled no runtime enforcement of policy boundaries

> This three-layer disconnect is where AI governance most commonly breaks down.

Why Policy Alone Fails

Policy-driven governance fails for structural reasons not because of bad intentions, but because of fundamental design limitations. Understanding these failure modes is essential before any solution can be designed.

1 **It Is Static**

Policies are written periodically. AI systems evolve continuously. The gap between them widens over time.

2 **It Is External**

Policies exist in documents and frameworks not within code or execution logic where behaviour is determined.

3 **It Assumes Compliance**

Policy assumes systems behave as intended. But AI systems adapt, drift, and encounter conditions no policy anticipated.

4 **No Real-Time Enforcement**

Policies do not monitor decisions, prevent actions, or trigger interventions at the moment they are needed most.

The Missing Layer: Control Systems

To bridge the gap between policy and execution, organisations need control systems mechanisms that translate intent into enforced behaviour at runtime. A control system in the AI context is a set of mechanisms embedded within the system that governs how decisions are made and actions are executed in real time.

Decision Boundaries

Define what an AI system can and cannot decide autonomously hard limits embedded in execution logic.

Threshold Mechanisms

Set confidence levels and risk limits that trigger different response paths depending on decision severity.

Enforcement Logic

Ensure policies are applied at runtime not assumed. Governance becomes code, not commentary.

Escalation Paths

Route critical decisions to human reviewers automatically, with defined criteria and audit trails.

Intervention Capabilities

Enable stopping or overriding system behaviour when it deviates from defined boundaries or exceeds risk thresholds.

From Oversight to Embedded Control

Traditional governance relies on oversight review processes, compliance checks, and periodic audits. Control systems fundamentally shift this model. The difference is not incremental; it is architectural. Governance must move from observation to enforcement.

Traditional Oversight Model

Governance as Documentation

Policies captured in written frameworks and guidelines

Policy as Guidance

Statements of intent, interpreted and applied inconsistently

Review After Action

Compliance assessed retrospectively through audits

Embedded Control Model

Governance as System Design

Control logic embedded within architecture and pipelines

Policy as Enforceable Logic

Constraints applied automatically at decision points

Control Before Action

Continuous enforcement operating during execution, in real time

Control as Architecture The Role of Engineering

Control cannot be added as an afterthought. It must be designed into system architecture from the outset. This requires identifying control points, embedding enforcement layers, and integrating monitoring and intervention capabilities into deployment pipelines and runtime behaviour.

This transition moves governance responsibility from legal and compliance functions into engineering and architecture. Engineers must now design control flows, decision constraints, and escalation mechanisms as first-class system requirements.

Design Phase

Identify control points and define enforcement logic during system architecture

Deployment Pipeline

Embed governance checks and validation gates before systems reach production

Runtime Behaviour

Continuously enforce boundaries, monitor decisions, and trigger escalations in live systems

ⓘ From trust and assumption to assurance, measurability, and accountability.

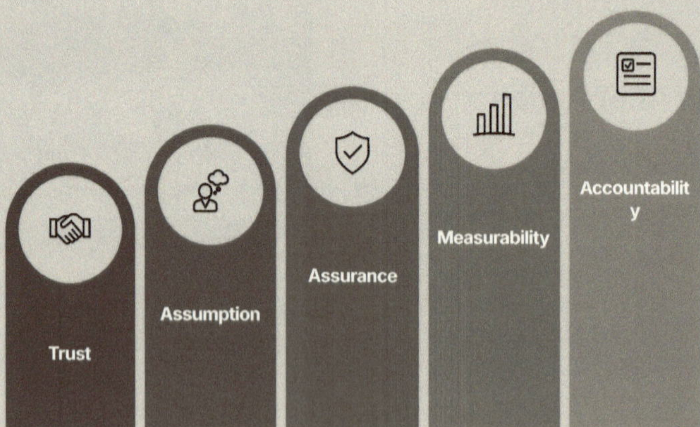

Key Takeaways & Looking Ahead

The central lesson of this chapter is clear: governance that lives only in documents is incomplete governance. Organisations must ask not *"Do we have AI governance?"* but *"Where is governance enforced in our systems?"* If the answer is unclear, governance is incomplete.

Policies define intent but do not enforce behaviour

Intent and execution are separate layers that require deliberate connection.

AI systems require runtime control, not just pre-deployment governance

Systems adapt and drift static policies cannot keep pace with live behaviour.

Control systems embed governance into decision-making

Boundaries, thresholds, enforcement logic, and escalation paths convert intent into action.

Governance must shift from documentation to architecture

Engineering teams must own control design as a core system responsibility.

> Policy tells the system what should happen. Control systems ensure it actually does. Without control, governance remains an idea. With control, it becomes reality.

Chapter 10

The Four-Layer Model of AI Control

Most organisations struggle with AI governance not because they lack intent but because they lack **structure**. Policies are written, processes are defined, and systems are deployed. Yet when decisions are executed, the connection between these elements breaks down. This chapter introduces a foundational construct that bridges intent and execution: **The Four-Layer Model of AI Control**.

Why Governance Breaks Down

Without a unifying model, AI governance fragments across the organisation. Intent lives in documents, processes sit in workflows, and systems operate independently none of them connected. The result is a structure that **cannot scale** and **cannot enforce** what it intends.

What Goes Wrong

- Gaps emerge between policy and execution
- Responsibilities become unclear
- Control becomes inconsistent
- Systems operate without alignment

What a Layered Model Provides

- Continuity from policy to execution
- Clear ownership at every level
- Modular, scalable control design
- A closed-loop governance system

⚠ Without structure, governance cannot scale. Without layers, control cannot be enforced.

The Four Layers at a Glance

The Four-Layer Model addresses all dimensions of AI system operation from strategic intent to human interaction. Each layer has distinct owners, tools, and operating speeds. Together, they form a **closed-loop control system**.

Policy

Define intent and boundaries

Process

Translate policy into workflows

Enforcement

Execute rules at runtime

Interface

Enable human oversight

Each layer serves a distinct purpose. None can be omitted without compromising the integrity of the whole.

Layer 1 Policy

FOUNDATION

The Policy Layer defines **intent and boundaries.** It is the origin point of all governance activity establishing the ethical principles, regulatory requirements, and organisational guidelines that every downstream layer must honour.

What It Includes

- Ethical principles
- Governance guidelines
- Regulatory requirements

Characteristics

- High-level and static
- Organisation-wide scope

Limitations

ⓘ Policy alone does not enforce behaviour. It requires active translation into actionable rules through the layers below it. A policy document sitting in a folder has no impact on a running AI system.

Layer 2 Process

TRANSLATION

The Process Layer **translates policy into operational workflows.** It is where abstract governance intent becomes concrete steps that teams and systems can follow approval chains, risk assessments, and escalation paths.

What It Includes

- Approval processes
- Risk assessment workflows
- Escalation procedures

Characteristics

- Semi-structured and role-based
- Designed to be repeatable

Limitations

⚠ Processes are often manual, not real-time, and can be bypassed under operational pressure. Without enforcement at the next layer, well-designed processes may never be followed in practice.

Layer 3 Enforcement ⭐

☆ MOST CRITICAL LAYER

Enforcement is the **most pivotal layer** in the entire model. It is where rules stop being theoretical and begin governing actual system behaviour in real time, automatically, and without relying on human memory or manual checks.

What It Includes

- Decision constraints
- Threshold checks
- Rule engines
- Control logic

Characteristics

- Embedded directly in systems
- Operates in real time
- Fully automated

Why It Matters

Without enforcement, policy and process have **no impact** on system behaviour. Systems operate autonomously. Governance remains entirely theoretical.

Layer 4 Interface

HUMAN OVERSIGHT

The Interface Layer **bridges human judgement and system execution**. It is the layer that makes AI governance visible and actionable giving operators, reviewers, and decision-makers the tools they need to observe, understand, and intervene.

What It Includes

- Dashboards and alerts
- Decision override mechanisms
- Explainability tools

Characteristics

- User-facing and interactive
- Context-aware

Role

The Interface Layer ensures that humans remain meaningfully in control not just nominally. It connects system outputs back to human judgement, completing the governance loop.

How the Layers Work Together

The Four-Layer Model is not a linear sequence it is an **interconnected, continuous control loop**. Each layer feeds into the next, and feedback flows back upward to refine policy over time. Consider how a high-risk financial transaction is governed end to end:

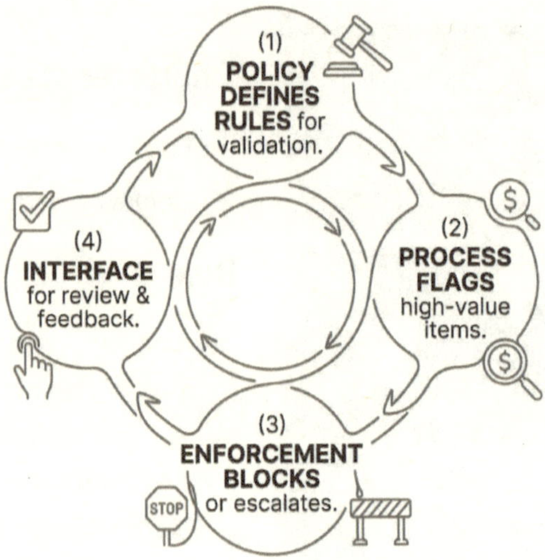

Together, these four stages form a governance system that is **operational, enforceable, and self-improving**.

Common Failure Patterns

Most governance breakdowns stem not from a single catastrophic failure but from **gaps between layers**. Each missing connection creates a category of incomplete governance that silently undermines control.

Policy Without Process

Intent exists in documents but has no operational translation. Good values never reach the teams or systems that need to act on them.

Process Without Enforcement

Workflows are defined but not enforced in systems. Compliance depends entirely on individual behaviour and breaks under pressure.

Enforcement Without Policy

Rules are implemented without alignment to organisational intent. Systems enforce constraints that no one deliberately designed or authorised.

Interface Without Control

Visibility exists, but there is no ability to intervene. Dashboards show problems that operators cannot fix governance theatre.

Each of these patterns produces the same result: governance that is incomplete, inconsistent, and ultimately unscalable.

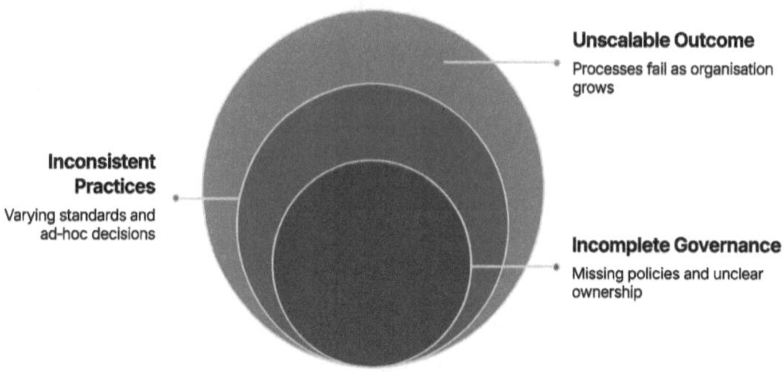

Designing Each Layer Effectively

Implementing the model requires deliberate design choices at every layer. Vagueness at any level propagates downward, creating gaps that undermine the whole system. Below are the key design imperatives for each layer.

Policy Layer

- Define clear, measurable rules
- Avoid ambiguity in principles

Process Layer

- Map workflows to system behaviour
- Ensure repeatability across roles

Enforcement Layer

- Embed logic directly into systems
- Use thresholds and hard constraints

Interface Layer

- Provide genuine visibility and context
- Enable meaningful intervention

The Feedback Loop & Scaling the Model

The Four-Layer Model is not static. A **continuous feedback loop** ensures that the system learns and improves over time with insights from the Interface Layer flowing back to refine Process and update Policy. This is what transforms governance from a compliance exercise into a living operational system.

The Feedback Loop

- Interface provides human insights
- Enforcement logs system behaviour
- Process is refined based on evidence
- Policy is updated to reflect learning

Scaling Across the Organisation

The model scales across teams, systems, and industries because it **separates concerns**, clarifies responsibilities, and enables modular design. Each layer can evolve independently without destabilising the others.

The Right Question

Instead of asking *"Do we have policies?"*, organisations must ask: *"Do our policies flow through all four layers?"* Only then does governance become operational, enforceable, and scalable.

Key Takeaways

Governance is not a single mechanism. It is a **system of layers working together**. When all four align, control becomes real. When even one is missing, governance becomes incomplete. The next chapter builds on this foundation to explore how decisions are bounded within this structure.

01

Governance requires structure to be effective

Intent alone is insufficient it must flow through all four layers.

02

Enforcement is the most critical layer

Without it, policy and process have no impact on actual system behaviour.

03

Gaps between layers create governance failure

Each disconnection produces a distinct, identifiable failure pattern.

04

The model creates a continuous control loop

Feedback ensures governance improves over time rather than becoming stale.

05

Next: Designing Decision Boundaries

Even with all four layers in place, systems need clearly defined limits for individual decisions.

> When all four layers align, control becomes real. When even one is missing, governance becomes incomplete.

Chapter 11

Designing Decision Boundaries

Every system technical or human operates within boundaries. Financial systems have limits. Networks have thresholds. Organisations have authority levels. AI systems, by default, have none of these. This chapter examines how to design explicit decision boundaries that transform AI from continuous execution engines into controlled, accountable decision systems.

The Core Challenge

Traditional systems are built with boundaries baked in. AI systems are built around data, objectives, and optimisation logic but unless explicitly designed, **they do not know where to stop.**

This is not a problem of intelligence or accuracy. It is an architectural gap: the absence of boundaries. Without them, all decisions are treated equally, and systems default to full automation regardless of risk, impact, or context.

> The core challenge of modern AI is not that it thinks poorly it is that it does not know when to stop thinking for itself.

What AI Systems Have by Default

- Data inputs and training objectives
- Optimisation logic
- Pattern recognition

What They Lack Without Design

- Limits on autonomous action
- Escalation conditions
- Context-sensitive constraints

What Are Decision Boundaries?

Decision boundaries define the limits within which an AI system can make decisions autonomously. They answer three critical operational questions that every deployed AI system must be able to resolve at runtime.

When Can It Act Freely?

Low-risk, reversible decisions with high model confidence that fall within routine operating parameters.

When Must It Pause?

Decisions approaching impact thresholds, exhibiting low confidence, or occurring in unusual contextual conditions.

When Must It Escalate?

High-impact, irreversible, or sensitive decisions that require human judgement, review, or authorisation.

ⓘ Without decision boundaries, every decision is treated with equal weight systems apply uniform logic to fundamentally non-uniform problems.

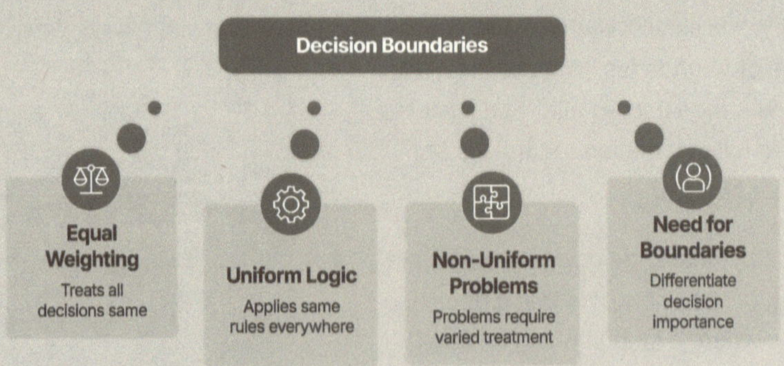

Four Dimensions of Decision Boundaries

Effective boundaries are not binary switches. They are defined across multiple dimensions that, in combination, determine how much autonomy is appropriate for any given decision.

Impact

Low → High
Determines the consequence of the decision and the downstream effects of an error.

Reversibility

Easy → Irreversible
Determines the ability to correct mistakes after the decision is executed.

Confidence

Low → High
Reflects the model's certainty in its output and the reliability of the underlying prediction.

Context Sensitivity

Standard → Complex
Captures the degree to which human judgement is required to interpret the situation correctly.

Decision Classification Framework

Combining these four dimensions produces a practical classification framework. Each category maps to a distinct control strategy, enabling differentiated responses across the full spectrum of AI decisions.

Category	Characteristics	Control Level
Routine	Low impact, reversible, high confidence	Full automation
Managed	Moderate impact, standard context	Controlled automation
Sensitive	High impact or low confidence	Human-in-the-loop
Critical	High impact, irreversible, complex context	Human decision required

This framework enables product teams to design differentiated control strategies rather than applying a single automation policy across all decision types.

Misclassification especially treating Sensitive or Critical decisions as Routine is a leading cause of AI governance failures in production systems.

Types of Decision Boundaries

Boundaries can be implemented in four distinct forms, each suited to different decision contexts and risk profiles. Most robust AI systems combine multiple types in layered configurations.

Threshold-Based

Define hard numeric limits transaction value, risk score, confidence level. When a threshold is exceeded, escalation is automatically triggered. Simplest to implement and audit.

Rule-Based

Define explicit conditional constraints: *"Do not approve above X without review"* or *"Block actions under condition Y."* Highly deterministic and traceable.

Contextual

Boundaries that adjust based on environment signals time of day, user behaviour patterns, or system state. Enables nuanced responses to situational factors.

Dynamic

Boundaries that adapt over time based on feedback loops and evolving risk levels. Most sophisticated requires ongoing monitoring and governance to prevent drift.

Boundary Placement in the Decision Flow

Boundaries must be embedded at multiple checkpoints across the entire decision lifecycle not just at the moment of action. Control applied at only one stage creates exploitable gaps.

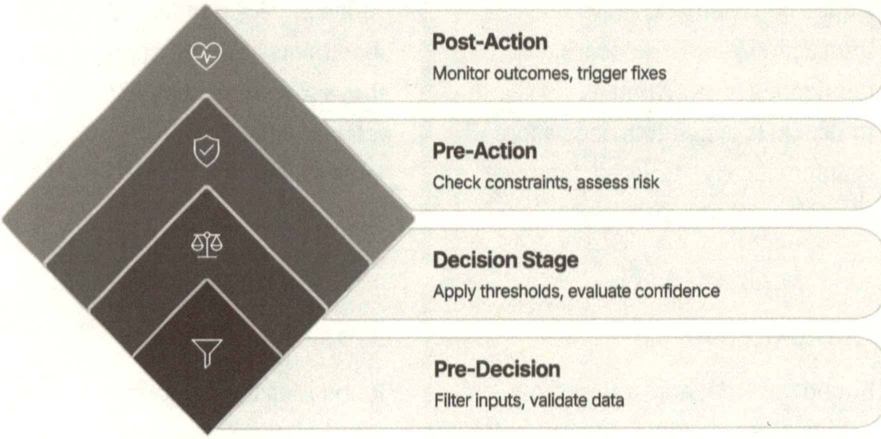

This four-stage embedding ensures that control is maintained from data ingestion through to outcome monitoring providing comprehensive governance across the full decision lifecycle rather than point-in-time checks.

Common Boundary Failures

Boundary design fails in predictable patterns. Understanding these failure modes is essential for AI system designers building production-grade decision systems.

Each failure type produces a distinct imbalance between control and performance either exposing the organisation to unnecessary risk, or undermining the operational value of automation entirely.

> The goal is not to eliminate autonomy. It is to enable **controlled autonomy** allowing AI to act where appropriate, and restricting it precisely where necessary.

Overly Broad

Too much autonomy; high risk exposure from unchecked decisions

Overly Restrictive

Excessive human intervention; automation value eliminated

Static

Fixed boundaries that fail to adapt as conditions and risk profiles change

Undefined

No explicit limits; system defaults to full automation by omission

Design Principles for Effective Boundaries

01

Explicit Definition

Boundaries must be clearly and unambiguously defined not implied or left to system defaults. Every boundary should be a deliberate design decision.

02

Measurability

Conditions that trigger boundary enforcement must be quantifiable. If a condition cannot be measured, it cannot be reliably enforced at runtime.

03

Enforceability

Boundaries must be embedded directly in system logic not documented separately and assumed to be followed. Policy without enforcement is not a boundary.

04

Adaptability

Boundaries must evolve with changing context, risk landscapes, and operational feedback. Static boundaries in dynamic environments become liabilities.

05

Transparency

Both the decisions made and the boundaries that govern them must be explainable to operators, auditors, and affected stakeholders.

Key Takeaways

→ Decision boundaries define the **limits of AI autonom** not all decisions should be automated equally

→ Boundaries must consider **impact, reversibility, confidence, and context sensitivity** in combination

→ Four boundary types — threshold, rule-based, contextual, and dynamic — are used in layered configurations

→ Boundaries must be enforced at **multiple points** in the decision flow, not just at the moment of action

→ The goal is **controlled autonomy** — enabling AI to act where appropriate, constrained where necessary

Chapter 12

Human-in-the-Loop vs Autonomous Systems

For years, the default answer to AI risk was simple: *"Keep a human in the loop."* It sounded safe. It sounded responsible. But as AI systems scaled to handle millions of decisions per second, this assumption began to break. The real question was never *whether* humans should be in the loop it is **where, when, and how** they should be placed.

Understanding the Spectrum of Control

Human involvement in AI systems is not binary. It exists across a continuous spectrum and most systems evolve along this spectrum over time, often without deliberate design. Recognising each model is the first step to deploying them intentionally.

Model	Definition	Typical Use Cases
Human-in-the-Loop (HITL)	Human reviews and approves decisions before execution	High-value financial decisions, regulatory-sensitive operations, safety-critical systems
Human-on-the-Loop (HOTL)	Human monitors system and intervenes when necessary	Network management, fraud monitoring, operational optimisation
Human-out-of-the-Loop (HOOTL)	System operates fully autonomously without direct oversight	Low-risk, high-frequency decisions, real-time optimisation

ⓘ Most systems drift toward greater autonomy over time often without a conscious governance decision being made.

A Closer Look at Each Model

Each control model carries distinct advantages and limitations. The appropriate model is never universal it depends on context, risk tolerance, and operational requirements.

Human-in-the-Loop (HITL)

Advantages: High control, clear accountability, reduced risk of unchecked errors.

Limitations: Slower execution, constrained scalability, significant operational cost. Fails when decision volume or speed is high.

Human-on-the-Loop (HOTL)

Advantages: Balances speed with oversight. Scalable across high-throughput environments while preserving intervention capability.

Limitations: Relies on effective monitoring infrastructure. Intervention may be delayed or reactive rather than preventive.

Human-out-of-the-Loop (HOOTL)

Advantages: Maximum speed and efficiency. Optimal for low-risk, repetitive, or time-critical decisions.

Limitations: No immediate intervention path. High risk if system boundaries are unclear or misaligned.

The Illusion of Human Control

Many organisations believe they have meaningful human oversight. In practice, the architecture tells a different story. Presence is confused with influence and monitoring is mistaken for control.

Humans Present

...but not empowered to act within the system's decision cycle.

Monitoring Exists

...but without the intervention capability to make it meaningful.

Alerts Generated

...but not acted upon in time to prevent downstream harm.

> The result is an illusion of control a governance structure that appears robust but lacks actual influence over outcomes.

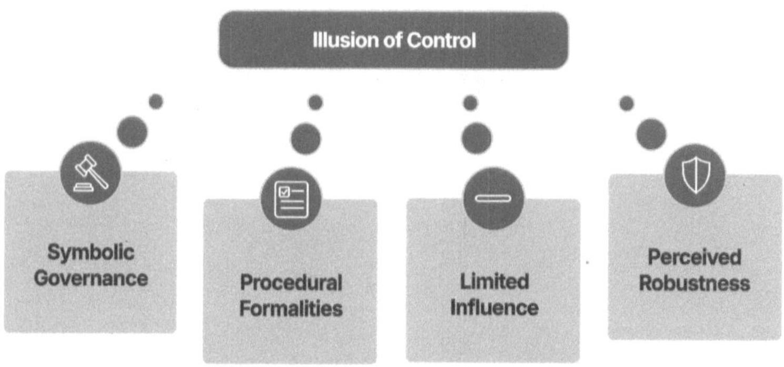

Why Full HITL Does Not Scale and Full Autonomy Introduces Risk

Why HITL Fails at Scale

AI systems operate at a pace and volume that humans fundamentally cannot match. Three compounding factors drive this breakdown:

- **Volume:** Thousands to millions of decisions generated continuously
- **Speed:** Decisions resolved in milliseconds
- **Complexity:** Each decision may require context, expertise, and rapid judgement

The outcome: human bottlenecks in high-throughput systems slowing delivery without improving safety.

Why Full Autonomy Increases Risk

At the opposite extreme, HOOTL systems remove the safeguards that catch misalignment before it compounds. Without a human check:

- No immediate intervention path exists
- No real-time validation of outputs
- Full reliance is placed on system logic alone

This can lead to overreach, accelerating misalignment, and amplified errors particularly in novel or edge-case scenarios the system was not designed to handle.

Strategic Human Placement: The Missing Design

The goal is not to choose between full human control and full automation. It is to embed human oversight **strategically** based on the nature of each decision, not blanket policy. Four criteria should govern placement.

1

Impact

High-impact decisions those affecting safety, finance, or regulatory compliance warrant direct human involvement before action is taken.

2

Reversibility

Irreversible decisions require human approval. Where consequences cannot be undone, autonomy is inappropriate regardless of confidence level.

3

Confidence

Low-confidence model outputs should automatically escalate. Systems must be designed to surface uncertainty not suppress it.

4

Context Complexity

Ambiguous or novel scenarios require human judgement. Autonomy is only appropriate where the decision space is well-defined and bounded.

Designing Effective Human Interaction

Human involvement must be **designed** not assumed. Without deliberate design, oversight becomes performative. Four structural elements are essential to making human involvement meaningful.

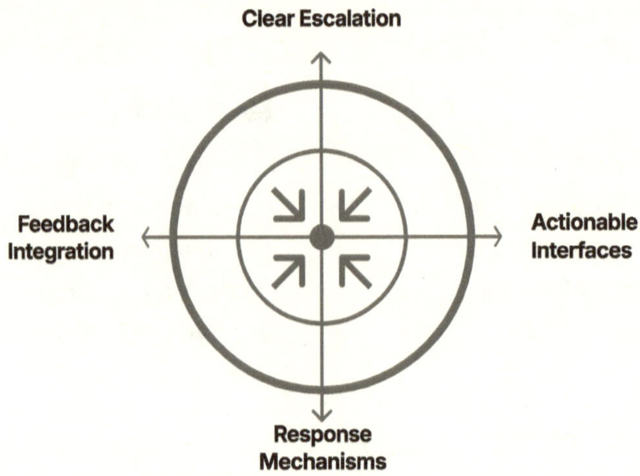

Critically, excessive human involvement creates its own risks. Decision fatigue, delayed responses, and reduced effectiveness can be as operationally dangerous as no involvement at all. Control is not about more humans it is about **smarter placement**.

> ⚠ Avoid human overload: routing too many decisions to humans degrades the quality of oversight, not just its speed.

The Future Model: Human–AI Collaboration

As AI systems mature, the human role fundamentally shifts from executing decisions to governing the systems that execute them. The most effective architecture is not human control *or* autonomy, but structured collaboration.

AI Handles	**Humans Handle**
Scale, speed, pattern recognition, and high-frequency low-risk decisions at operational throughput.	Judgement, exceptions, ethical boundaries, and governance of system behaviour over time.

> The strength of a system is not in how much it automates but in how intelligently it knows when to involve a human.

- Human involvement exists across a spectrum: HITL, HOTL, and HOOTL
- Full human control does not scale; full autonomy amplifies risk
- Placement decisions should be driven by impact, reversibility, confidence, and context
- Effective oversight requires clear escalation paths, actionable interfaces, and feedback loops
- The goal is collaboration not replacement. AI systems redefine the human role, they do not eliminate it.

Looking Ahead: Even with well-designed human placement, systems must operate under embedded constraints. Chapter 13 explores **Control Points in AI Systems** how oversight is architecturally enforced, not merely assumed.

Chapter 13

Control Points in AI Systems

Most organisations ask: *"Do we have control over our AI system?"* A better question is: *"Where exactly is control applied?"* Control is not a single switch, a policy, or a dashboard. It is a series of deliberate intervention points embedded across the system and without them, decisions flow uninterrupted, actions execute automatically, and risks propagate silently.

What Are Control Points?

Definition

Control points are **specific locations within an AI system** where behaviour can be influenced, constrained, or overridden. They are not passive monitors they are active intervention mechanisms built into the architecture of the system itself.

Control is not about having authority. It is about having the **ability to intervene** at the right point, at the right time.

What Control Points Enable

→ **Validate Inputs**

Ensure data entering the pipeline meets quality and integrity standards before processing begins.

→ **Evaluate Decisions**

Assess model outputs and apply business logic before any decision is confirmed.

→ **Prevent Incorrect Actions**

Block or escalate actions that violate policy, exceed risk thresholds, or lack sufficient confidence.

→ **Monitor Outcomes**

Track results post-execution and feed validated signals back into the system.

The AI System Flow

To design control points effectively, you must first understand the pipeline. Every AI system transforms data through a series of stages and each stage introduces potential risk that requires deliberate control.

Without control points, this pipeline operates as a continuous, uninterrupted flow no validation, no constraint, no opportunity to intervene. With control points, each stage becomes a governed checkpoint where behaviour can be evaluated, adjusted, or halted.

Types of Control Points

Control points are categorised by their position in the pipeline. Each type serves a distinct purpos and no single type is sufficient on its own. Effective governance requires coverage across all six stages.

Input Control Points

Pre-processing. Validate data quality, filter anomalies, and detect outliers before any model sees the data. Garbage in means garbage out flawed input produces flawed decisions downstream.

Model Control Points

Inference stage. Check confidence levels, detect anomalous predictions, and apply calibration. Even accurate models produce uncertain outputs not every prediction should be trusted equally.

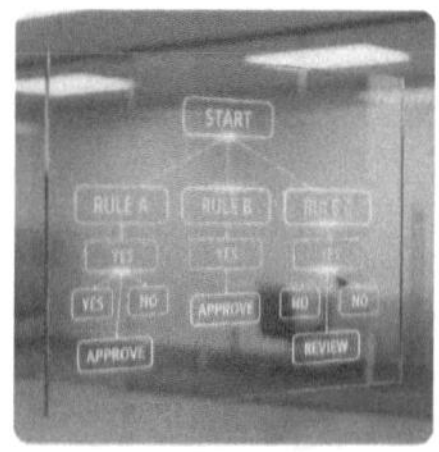

Decision Control Points

Logic layer. Apply business rules, evaluate thresholds, and classify decision risk. This is where insight becomes intent decisions must be bounded, not blindly executed.

Control Points: Action, Post-Action & Feedback

Action Control Points

Pre-execution. Validate whether a decision should be executed. Check policy compliance, evaluate risk conditions, and trigger escalation if required.

⚠ This is the final checkpoint before real-world impact. Once action is taken, reversal may not be possible.

Post-Action Control Points

Monitoring. Track outcomes, detect anomalies in system behaviour, and log all decisions for auditability. Provides the raw data for correction and continuous improvement.

Feedback Control Points

Learning validation. Ensure feedback signals are accurate and prevent the reinforcement of incorrect behaviour. Feedback loops can *amplify* errors if left uncontrolled.

Control Coverage Across the System

An effective AI governance framework ensures that every stage of the pipeline has a corresponding control point. The table below maps stages to their controls and highlights where gaps most commonly emerge.

Stage	Control Point	Common Gap
Data Ingestion	Input data validation	Focused only on format, not semantic quality
Model Inference	Confidence & anomaly checks	No calibration; all outputs treated equally
Decision Logic	Rule enforcement & thresholds	Direct mapping from model output to action
Action Execution	Risk & compliance validation	No escalation trigger; actions auto-execute
Post-Action	Outcome monitoring & logging	Detection only no prevention capability
Feedback Loop	Learning signal validation	Incorrect patterns reinforced over time

⊗ Partial control is not control. Each unaddressed gap creates an uncontrolled pathway within the system where risk can propagate without detection or intervention.

Design Principles for Control Points

Well-designed control points do not create bottlenecks they operate with minimal latency, using thresholds and automation to govern behaviour in real time. The goal is **control without friction**. These five principles guide effective control point design.

1

Placement Precision

Control must exist at critical stages of the pipeline not applied uniformly, but positioned where risk is highest and intervention has the most leverage.

2

Minimal Latency

Decisions should not be delayed unnecessarily. Control logic must be lightweight and optimised for real-time operation at production throughput.

3

Clear Trigger Conditions

Define explicitly when control is applied through thresholds, rule sets, or anomaly signals so that governance is consistent and predictable.

4

Escalation Capability

Enable human intervention when automated controls are insufficient. Not every edge case can be anticipated escalation paths are a design requirement, not an afterthought.

5

Observability

Ensure every control action is traceable. If you cannot audit what the control point did and why, governance cannot be demonstrated or improved.

From Continuous Flow to Controlled Flow

Without Control Points

Continuous Pipeline

Unrestricted execution data flows through every stage without interruption, validation, or constraint.

Passive Processing

The system transforms inputs to outputs automatically. Risk propagates silently across all stages.

No Intervention Opportunity

By the time a problem is visible, action has already been taken and may be irreversible.

With Control Points

Segmented Pipeline

Controlled execution each stage is a governed checkpoint with defined behaviour and escalation paths.

Actively Governed System

The system validates, evaluates, and conditionally executes transforming passive processing into deliberate decision-making.

Intervention at Every Stage

Control is exercised before, during, and after action enabling correction, escalation, and audit at each point.

> Control is not about watching systems. It is about shaping their behaviour at specific points, deliberately designed and carefully placed. **If you cannot identify your control points, you do not control your system.**

The next chapter explores **Runtime Guardrails** how control is enforced in real time, because detection alone is not enough. Systems must actively constrain behaviour as it unfolds.

Chapter 14

Runtime Guardrails

AI systems do not stop at deployment they operate continuously, making decisions under live conditions. This chapter examines how runtime guardrails enforce control during execution, bridging the gap between design assumptions and real-world behaviour.

The Control Gap

Most organisations design control for the **beginning** of the AI lifecycle. Data is validated, models are tested, systems are approved — then deployed. From that moment, the system operates continuously, and behaviour is assumed rather than enforced.

The Assumption

"The system will behave as expected."

Pre-deployment validation is treated as sufficient. Stable data, known conditions, and predictable behaviour are taken for granted.

The Reality

AI systems operate in dynamic environments. They encounter new data, unexpected scenarios, and shifting contexts — none of which were present during testing.

- Data drift alters input distributions
- Edge cases trigger unvalidated behaviour
- Emergent outputs diverge from expectations

⚠ Control cannot stop at deployment. It must exist at runtime.

What Are Runtime Guardrails?

Runtime guardrails are **real-time constraints and checks embedded within AI systems** that govern behaviour during execution. Unlike policies or pre-deployment reviews, guardrails are active, continuous, and enforceable — operating on every decision, under live conditions.

Active	Continuous	Enforceable
Operate while the system is running, not after the fact	Applied to every decision across the full execution lifecycle	Embedded in system logic — not advisory, but binding

Why Guardrails Are Necessary

AI systems learn, adapt, and generalise. This dynamism is a strength — and a source of uncertainty. Even well-trained models encounter unseen inputs, produce low-confidence outputs, or operate outside expected conditions. Guardrails ensure systems remain within acceptable limits regardless of what they encounter.

The case for guardrails is not a failure of model quality — it is an acknowledgement that no validation process can anticipate every real-world condition. Guardrails are the mechanism by which design intent is preserved at runtime.

Design vs. Reality

Pre-deployment validation operates under controlled assumptions. Runtime reality is fundamentally different. This gap is where risk accumulates — and where guardrails intervene.

Phase	Assumption	Runtime Reality
Design	Controlled conditions	Dynamic, shifting environments
Testing	Known scenarios	Unknown edge cases
Deployment	Expected behaviour	Emergent, unpredicted behaviour

> Guardrails bridge the gap between what was designed and what is executed.

Types of Runtime Guardrails

Guardrails can be implemented across five distinct categories, each targeting a different dimension of risk during system execution.

1

Threshold-Based

Limit decisions based on predefined confidence or risk scores. Prevents low-certainty outputs from being executed.

2

Rule-Based

Explicit policy constraints embedded in system logic. Blocks actions under defined conditions without exception.

3

Context-Aware

Adjusts thresholds and rules based on operational environment — user segment, system load, or situational factors.

4

Anomaly Detection

Identifies unusual patterns in inputs or outputs in real time, triggering alerts or halts when behaviour deviates.

5

Rate-Limiting

Caps the frequency of actions to prevent cascading failures from high-volume or repeated decisions.

Where Guardrails Operate

Effective guardrail architecture places controls across every key stage of the decision and action lifecycle — not solely at the point of output.

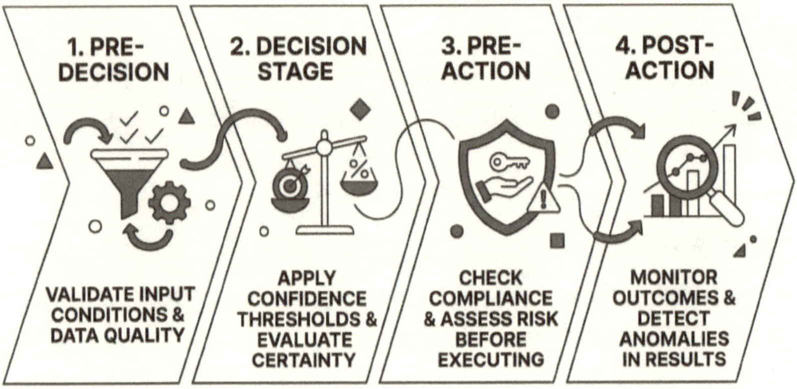

This end-to-end placement ensures that control is continuous — not a single checkpoint, but an integrated layer of enforcement across the entire execution path.

Guardrails vs. Monitoring

These two mechanisms are frequently conflated, but serve fundamentally different functions:

Aspect	Monitoring	Guardrails
Timing	After action	Before or during action
Function	Observe and record	Prevent and constrain
Impact	Reactive	Proactive

ⓘ Monitoring tells you what happened. Guardrails control what happens.

Design Principles & The Cost of Failure

Guardrails must be designed with discipline. Both extremes carry risk: over-restriction degrades system utility, while under-restriction exposes the organisation to uncontrolled execution at scale.

Principles for Effective Guardrails

→ **Real-Time Execution**

Operate without delay — latency undermines enforceability

→ **Clear Trigger Conditions**

Define precisely when and why a guardrail activates

→ **Enforceability**

Embedded in system logic, not advisory documentation

→ **Adaptability**

Adjust dynamically to changing operational conditions

Failure Without Guardrails

Low-confidence outputs are executed

Systems act on uncertain predictions without constraint

Edge cases trigger incorrect actions

Unvalidated scenarios produce harmful downstream effects

Drift goes undetected

Feedback loops reinforce and amplify erroneous behaviour

Uncontrolled execution at scale

Risk compounds with every unconstrained decision cycle

> Guardrails are the first line of defence in AI control systems — immediate protection, continuous enforcement, and active risk mitigation at runtime.

Looking Ahead: Guardrails prevent incorrect actions. But what happens when guardrails fail, unexpected conditions arise, or immediate intervention is required? The next chapter explores **Kill Switches & Escalation Mechanisms** — the tools that enable systems to stop, escalate, and recover.

Chapter 15

Kill Switches & Escalation

Every high-stakes system in the physical world has one critical feature: **a way to stop.** AI systems are often designed without this principle continuing to operate, decide, and execute even when behaviour becomes questionable. This chapter examines the mechanisms that restore control when it matters most.

Why Stopping Matters

The Problem

AI systems operate continuously processing data, generating decisions, and triggering actions at scale and speed. When something goes wrong, errors propagate quickly, impact spreads across systems, and recovery becomes complex.

Without intervention mechanisms, organisations are forced to **observe failure** instead of preventing it.

The Principle

Power grids have circuit breakers. Aircraft have override controls. Industrial systems have emergency shutdowns. These mechanisms exist for one reason: when systems behave unexpectedly, control must be immediate.

⚠ If a system cannot be stopped, it is not controlled.

The Role of Kill Switches

A kill switch is a mechanism that immediately halts or restricts system behaviour under defined conditions. Far from being a sign of weakness, kill switches are a necessary component of resilient systems.

Immediate Control

Halt problematic behaviour the moment it is detected no delay, no drift.

Risk Containment

Prevent errors from propagating across interconnected systems and processes.

System Reset

Enable rollback and controlled restart after investigation and remediation.

Types of Kill Switches

Kill switches operate at different levels of granularity, allowing organisations to match intervention scope to the severity of the issue.

1

System-Level

Stops the entire AI system. Used for critical failure or widespread incorrect behaviour. Maximum containment highest disruption.

2

Function-Level

Disables specific functionalities. Targets a faulty module or incorrect decision logic whilst keeping the broader system operational.

3

Decision-Level

Blocks specific decisions particularly high-risk transactions or sensitive actions. Enables granular, surgical control.

4

Conditional

Activates automatically based on predefined conditions: confidence below threshold, anomaly detected, or policy violation triggered.

Escalation as Complement to Kill Switches

Stopping is not always the best response. In many cases, decisions require review, context, and human judgement. Escalation mechanisms ensure that critical cases are handled appropriately rather than systems operating blindly.

Threshold-Based

Triggered when risk exceeds a defined limit or confidence falls below an acceptable level.

Rule-Based

Triggered by policy conditions or regulatory requirements that mandate human review.

Contextual

Triggered by complex or ambiguous inputs where automated decision-making is insufficient.

Anomaly-Based

Triggered by unusual patterns or unexpected outputs that deviate from established norms.

Kill Switch vs. Escalation

Both mechanisms are essential they serve complementary roles within a controlled AI system. Kill switches prevent damage; escalation enables resolution.

Mechanism	Primary Purpose	Outcome
Kill Switch	Stop system behaviour immediately	Containment, reset capability
Escalation	Transfer decision to a human	Informed resolution, accountability

Designing Effective Kill Switches

- **Clear trigger conditions** define when and at what thresholds
- **Immediate execution** no delay in halting behaviour
- **Controlled impact limit** disruption where possible
- **Recoverability** allow restart or rollback

Designing Effective Escalation

- **Timely** triggered before impact occurs
- **Context-rich** provide information for sound decisions
- **Actionable** enable approval, rejection, or modification
- **Integrated** seamlessly connected to system workflow

Layered Intervention Strategy

Effective AI governance does not rely on a single point of control. Kill switches and escalation operate as part of a broader layered defence each layer addressing a different category of risk.

1

Guardrails

Prevent incorrect actions before they occur

2

Escalation

Handle uncertain decisions with human judgement

3

Kill Switches

Stop critical failures immediately

ⓘ Kill switches connect to the **Enforcement Layer** for runtime control; escalation connects to the **Interface Layer** for human interaction together bridging system behaviour and human decision-making.

Common Failure Patterns & Key Takeaways

Where Organisations Fail

No Kill Switch

System continues operating despite clear failure signals.

Delayed Activation

Response arrives after damage has already propagated.

Overuse

Frequent shutdowns erode system effectiveness and trust.

Weak Escalation

Decisions routed without context humans cannot act effectively.

Key Takeaways

- → Kill switches provide **immediate control** over system behaviour
- → Escalation enables **human intervention** for critical decisions
- → Four kill switch levels: System, Function, Decision, Conditional
- → Four escalation types: Threshold, Rule, Contextual, Anomaly
- → Together they form a **layered control strategy**

> True control is not about preventing all failures. It is about knowing when and how to stop.

Chapter 16

Observability & Auditability

You cannot control what you cannot see. In traditional systems, visibility was straightforward rules were explicit, logic was deterministic, and outputs were predictable. AI systems change this completely. Decisions are no longer transparent by default, yet they affect customers, trigger actions, and drive outcomes. Without visibility, behaviour cannot be understood, risk cannot be assessed, and accountability cannot be assigned. **Control without visibility is an illusion.**

From Monitoring to Observability

Organisations often believe they have visibility because they monitor their systems. But monitoring and observability are fundamentally different disciplines that answer different questions.

Monitoring

Tracks metrics, performance indicators, and system health.

> "What is happening?"

Monitoring is **reactive** it alerts you when something has already gone wrong.

Observability

Understands system behaviour through outputs, logs, and internal signals.

> "Why is it happening?"

Observability is **diagnostic** it gives you the context to understand root cause and systemic behaviour in AI systems that adapt and evolve over time.

Two Foundational Concepts

Effective governance of AI systems rests on two complementary pillars. Neither is sufficient alone together they form the basis of trustworthy, accountable AI operations.

Observability

The ability to understand system behaviour through its outputs, logs, and internal signals. Observability provides insight into decisions, context for actions, and visibility into system state *as they happen*.

Auditability

The ability to trace, reconstruct, and validate decisions *after they occur*. Auditability ensures accountability, compliance, and verifiability enabling organisations to demonstrate control to regulators and stakeholders.

ⓘ Together, observability and auditability enable **trust, control, and accountability** across the full lifecycle of AI decision-making.

Key Components of Observability

An effective observability strategy is built from four interlocking components. Each addresses a distinct layer of visibility, from raw data capture through to human-interpretable reasoning.

Logging

Captures system activity inputs, model outputs, decisions, and actions. Provides the raw data foundation for all subsequent analysis.

Metrics

Tracks performance indicators such as accuracy, latency, and error rates. Shows trends but does not reveal root cause on its own.

Tracing

Follows the decision flow across the system tracking data paths, processing steps, and decision logic to show how outcomes are produced.

Explainability

Provides reasoning behind decisions through feature importance and model interpretation. Helps humans understand system behaviour at a conceptual level.

Key Components of Auditability

Auditability transforms observability data into structured, verifiable records. It is the mechanism by which organisations demonstrate accountability and meet regulatory obligations.

Decision Records

Capture what decision was made, when it was made, and under what conditions creating an immutable audit trail for every consequential output.

Version Tracking

Track model version, data version, and system configuration at the time of each decision. Essential for understanding how system changes affect behaviour.

Policy Mapping

Link decisions to applicable policies and governance rules, enabling organisations to demonstrate that outputs align with stated controls and standards.

Reproducibility

The ability to recreate decisions and validate outcomes. Reproducibility is the ultimate test of auditability if a decision cannot be reconstructed, it cannot be verified.

The Observability Stack

No single component provides complete visibility. An effective observability system layers these capabilities so that each layer informs and enriches the others, providing a complete picture of system behaviour.

Layer	Function	Answers
Logs	Raw data capture	What occurred?
Metrics	Performance tracking	How is it performing?
Tracing	Flow visibility	How did it happen?
Explainability	Decision reasoning	Why did it happen?

> The power of the observability stack lies in **integration**. Metrics alert you to a problem; tracing shows you where it originated; logs supply the evidence; explainability reveals the cause. Together they close the loop from symptom to root cause.

Common Observability Gaps

Despite the availability of observability tooling, organisations frequently fall short in practice. These gaps silently erode visibility and weaken control often without teams realising it until a failure occurs.

Incomplete Logging

Missing critical data and inconsistent capture leave blind spots in the audit trail. If it was not logged, it cannot be investigated.

Metric Overreliance

Focusing solely on performance metrics while ignoring behavioural signals. Systems can perform well by narrow measures while exhibiting harmful drift.

Lack of Traceability

Inability to follow a decision through the full system path. When something goes wrong, the cause cannot be located or attributed.

Limited Explainability

Black-box decisions that cannot be interpreted by humans. Opaque outputs make it impossible to assess fairness, accuracy, or appropriateness.

⚠ These gaps do not merely reduce visibility they **create unacceptable regulatory and operational risk** in high-stakes AI deployments.

Observability as a Control Mechanism

Observability is not merely a diagnostic tool it is an active component of the AI control architecture. Without observability, control mechanisms operate blindly, reacting only after harm has occurred. Regulators increasingly require decision transparency, traceability, and accountability, making auditability an operational necessity rather than a governance aspiration.

Observability Enables

- Real-time detection of anomalous behaviour
- Triggering of automated guardrails
- Activating escalation and human review
- Evidence for regulatory demonstration

Balancing Transparency & Complexity

Full transparency is not always achievable in complex AI systems. The goal is **sufficient explainability** not complete simplification. Systems must be understandable enough to govern, audit, and trust, without demanding that every probabilistic inference be reduced to a simple rule.

From Black Box to Glass Box

With robust observability and auditability in place, AI systems shift from opaque black boxes to sufficiently transparent glass boxes not perfectly visible, but understandable enough to govern, control, and trust. This visibility is the foundation for all structured AI control frameworks.

Observability provides real-time visibility into system behaviour

Through logging, metrics, tracing, and explainability working together as an integrated stack.

Auditability enables traceability and post-hoc accountability

Via decision records, version tracking, policy mapping, and reproducibility.

Monitoring is reactive observability is diagnostic

The distinction is critical: one tells you something went wrong, the other tells you why.

Observability is the precondition for effective control

Without it, guardrails, escalation, and governance mechanisms operate blindly. The next step is the AI Control Maturity Model.

> AI systems are powerful but complex. Control begins with seeing clearly. And seeing clearly requires systems designed to be understood

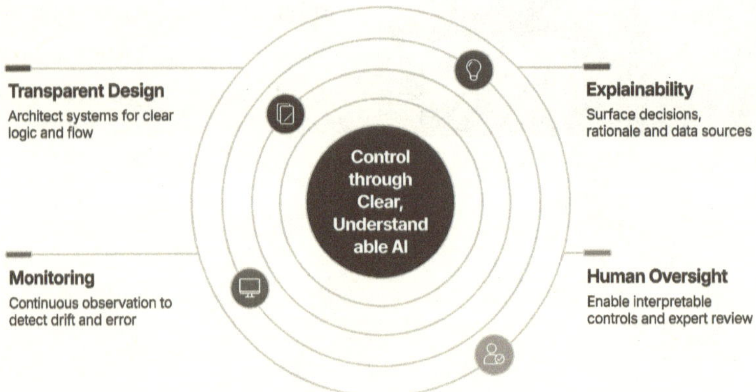

Chapter 17

The AI Control Maturity Model

Every organisation believes it is progressing with AI — more models deployed, more automation achieved, more decisions optimised. But a critical question is rarely asked: **How mature is our control over these systems?** AI maturity is not just about capability. It is about control over capability.

The Illusion of Progress

Two organisations may use similar models and operate at similar scale — yet differ fundamentally in risk exposure, decision reliability, and governance strength. Progress measured only in accuracy, speed, and scale masks a deeper question about control.

Traditional Measurement

- Accuracy of predictions
- Speed of deployment
- Scale of automation

These metrics tell you *how capable* your AI is.

What's Actually Missing

- Risk exposure assessment
- Decision reliability measures
- Governance strength indicators

Without these, organisations scale AI — but **not control**. The difference lies in control maturity.

What Is the AI Control Maturity Model?

The AI Control Maturity Model is a structured framework that defines how effectively an organisation governs, controls, and manages AI-driven decision systems. It serves as both a mirror and a map — showing where you are and guiding where you need to go.

Diagnostic Tool

Identify your current level of control maturity with clarity and precision.

Benchmarking Framework

Compare your control posture against industry peers and standards.

Transformation Roadmap

Define a structured path for advancing governance and control capabilities.

Why Maturity Matters

AI systems evolve. Organisations evolve. But without a maturity model, progress remains unstructured, gaps stay hidden, and investments become misaligned with actual risk. A maturity model brings discipline and direction to an otherwise ad hoc journey.

Without a Maturity Model

- Progress is unstructured and unmeasurable
- Critical governance gaps remain hidden
- Investment decisions are misaligned with risk

With a Maturity Model

- Clear positioning within a defined spectrum
- Targeted improvement with measurable outcomes
- Structured advancement through validated levels

A maturity model does not constrain AI ambition — it ensures that ambition is matched by proportionate control.

The Six Levels of AI Control Maturity

The model defines six levels, each representing a distinct stage in the evolution of organisational control over AI systems. Progression is not automatic — it requires deliberate investment in governance, architecture, and enforcement.

Level	Name	System Behaviour	Risk Profile	Typical Org
Level 0	Uncontrolled	AI acts without constraints or escalation	Extremely High	Early adopters
Level 1	Aware	Limited manual oversight, monitoring begins	High	Policy-intent orgs
Level 2	Defined	Partial control, some escalation paths	Moderate–High	Documenting orgs
Level 3	Enforced	Decisions constrained, escalation active	Moderate	Governed orgs
Level 4	Adaptive	Boundaries adapt, feedback loops active	Low	Mature orgs
Level 5	Autonomous Control	AI manages its own boundaries intelligently	Controlled	Leading orgs

Deep Dive: Levels 0 to 2

The foundational levels represent the earliest stages of control maturity — from complete absence of governance to the emergence of defined processes. Understanding these levels is essential for honest self-assessment.

Level 0 — Uncontrolled

No formal governance. AI acts without constraints, no escalation mechanisms exist. Risk is extremely high. Common in organisations that deployed rapidly without structural oversight.

Level 1 — Aware

Awareness of AI risk exists. Policies and guidelines are drafted, but limited manual oversight means governance exists in intent — not in execution. Policies are not enforced.

Level 2 — Defined

Processes are documented, decision categories are defined, and partial control mechanisms are in place. Control is designed — but inconsistently applied across the organisation.

Deep Dive: Levels 3 to 5

The advanced levels represent genuine operational maturity — where control is not aspirational but embedded, enforced, and eventually self-managing. These levels are the target state for organisations with significant AI risk exposure.

Level 3 — Enforced

Control systems are embedded. Runtime guardrails are active, escalation mechanisms are operational, and governance is enforceable. Risk is reduced to moderate — enforcement is the differentiator.

Level 4 — Adaptive

Dynamic control mechanisms respond to changing conditions. Boundaries adapt to context, feedback loops are validated, and the system evolves with continuous monitoring. Risk profile is low.

Level 5 — Autonomous Control

Self-regulating systems with embedded governance. AI manages its own boundaries and escalates intelligently. High efficiency with controlled, optimised risk. The pinnacle of control maturity.

Dimensions of Maturity

Maturity is not a single-axis measurement. It is evaluated across five interconnected dimensions, each contributing to the overall control posture of an organisation's AI systems.

Each dimension must advance in concert. Organisations that focus exclusively on one dimension — such as system architecture — while neglecting governance or observability will plateau and face compounding risk.

Progression, Pitfalls & Application

Progression Path

01

0 → 1: Recognise

Acknowledge AI risk and define initial policies.

02

1 → 2: Formalise

Document processes and categorise decisions.

03

2 → 3: Enforce

Embed guardrails and implement runtime controls.

04

3 → 4: Adapt

Introduce dynamic control and continuous monitoring.

05

4 → 5: Automate

Enable self-regulating, intelligent control systems.

Common Pitfalls

Overestimating Maturity

Policies are mistaken for active control. Documentation is not enforcement.

Skipping Levels

Attempting advanced control without foundational governance creates fragility.

Technology-Only Focus

Ignoring process and governance dimensions leaves critical gaps exposed.

Underinvesting in Enforcement

Weak runtime control renders even well-designed governance ineffective.

Reframing AI Maturity

Traditional View

More AI → Higher Maturity

Maturity is equated with capability: more models, more automation, more scale. Control is assumed to follow naturally from deployment.

The New View

> More Control → Higher Maturity

Maturity is defined by the quality of governance over AI systems. Capability without control is not progress — it is compounding risk. The most mature organisations are those with the strongest control intelligence.

The goal is not simply to build more capable AI systems. The goal is to build **controlled, scalable AI systems** — where capability and governance advance in lockstep.

Assess

Identify your current maturity level honestly and precisely.

Benchmark

Compare your control posture against industry peers.

Roadmap

Define your structured transformation path level by level.

Report

Communicate maturity progress clearly to stakeholders.

Key Takeaways

Chapter 17 establishes the AI Control Maturity Model as the foundational lens through which all AI governance should be evaluated. The next chapter explores the characteristics of each maturity level in greater operational detail.

Control Defines Maturity

AI maturity is not about capability — it is about how effectively that capability is governed and controlled.

Six Levels, One Spectrum

From Uncontrolled (Level 0) to Autonomous Control (Level 5), each level represents increasing control and reduced risk exposure.

Five Dimensions, One Score

Governance, decision control, architecture, observability, and adaptability must all advance together for genuine maturity.

Structured Advancement is Non-Negotiable

Skipping levels, mistaking policy for enforcement, or focusing only on technology are the most common and costly pitfalls.

> AI systems will continue to evolve. The question is whether control evolves with them. Maturity is not defined by how advanced your AI is — it is defined by how well you control it.

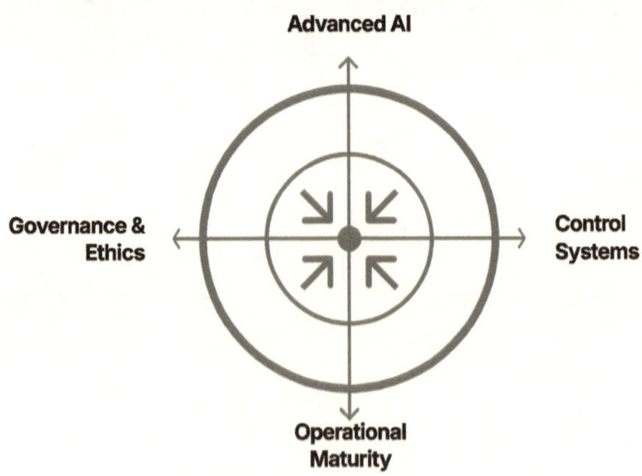

Chapter 18

Characteristics of Each Maturity Level

A maturity model is only useful if it can be applied. This chapter translates abstract levels into observable reality defining what each stage actually looks like in system behaviour, governance posture, and human involvement. **You don't determine maturity by what you intend. You determine it by how your systems actually operate.**

From Levels to Reality

Each maturity level reflects a distinct operating model, a specific risk posture, and a different relationship between humans and AI systems. Maturity is visible not theoretical. It manifests in four observable dimensions that cut across every level of the framework.

System Behaviour

How the AI operates at runtime what it does, what it constrains, and how it responds to edge conditions.

Decision Patterns

Whether decisions are bounded, escalated, or unconstrained and who or what is accountable for each.

Control Mechanisms

The guardrails, enforcement points, and runtime rules that translate policy into system behaviour.

Organisational Practices

How teams govern, intervene, escalate, and review the human infrastructure surrounding the system.

Levels 0 & 1 Uncontrolled and Aware

The earliest stages of maturity are characterised by an absence of effective control. Organisations at these levels may understand risk intellectually, but lack the mechanisms to act on that understanding in a consistent or timely way.

Level 0 Uncontrolled

No defined decision boundaries. Model output maps directly to action with no guardrails or constraints. Human involvement is minimal or absent. Observability is limited or nonexistent.

- Continuous, unrestricted execution
- Frequent anomalies and unpredictable outcomes
- Very high exposure with no detection capability

System acts without awareness of limits.

Level 1 Aware

Initial monitoring is in place and some manual checks exist. Policies are defined and guidelines documented, but intervention is reactive issues are detected after they occur, not prevented.

- Mostly automated, occasionally reviewed
- Basic metrics tracked
- Issues detected after occurrence
- Risk understood but not effectively controlled

Organisation understands the risk but cannot control it effectively.

Level 2 Defined

At Level 2, control is designed but not yet consistently enforced. Decision categories are identified, partial boundary definitions exist, and human-in-the-loop mechanisms are introduced for select high-stakes decisions. This level is frequently misidentified as more mature than it is.

System Characteristics

Decision categories identified. Partial boundary definitions in place. Mixed automation with controlled segments.

Governance

Processes documented and approval workflows defined but enforcement is inconsistent across teams and systems.

Human Involvement

Human-in-the-loop introduced for select decisions. Structured monitoring established, though gaps remain between design and execution.

Risk Indicators

Inconsistent enforcement. Gaps between documented design and actual execution remain a primary vulnerability.

⚠ Control is designed but not consistently enforced. Documentation alone does not constitute Level 2 maturity.

Level 3 Enforced

Level 3 represents the first stage where control is genuinely operational. Guardrails are embedded at runtime, policies are translated into system rules, and escalation mechanisms are structured rather than ad hoc. System behaviour becomes predictable and anomalies are significantly reduced.

System

Control points embedded. Runtime guardrails active. Conditional decision-making enforced.

Governance

Policies translated directly into system rules. Not merely documented enforced.

Human Role

Structured escalation mechanisms. Human involvement is triggered by defined conditions, not intuition.

Observability

Comprehensive logging and tracing. Decisions are auditable and traceable end-to-end.

Control is operational and enforced at runtime. Anomalies are reduced and system behaviour becomes predictable.

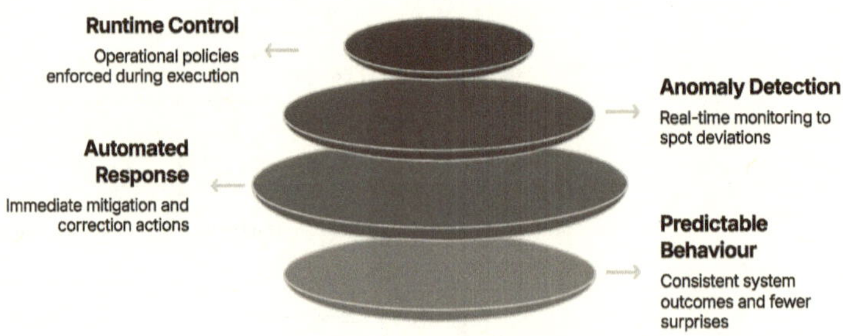

Levels 4 & 5 Adaptive and Autonomous Control

The upper levels of the maturity framework represent fundamentally different operating paradigms. Control evolves from static enforcement to dynamic adaptation, and ultimately to systems that govern themselves with embedded intelligence and full transparency.

Level 4 Adaptive

Dynamic boundaries respond to context. Governance is continuously updated through feedback-driven refinement. Human involvement shifts to strategic oversight rather than operational intervention.

- Real-time insights and drift detection
- Systems adjust to changing conditions
- Early issue detection and rapid response
- Risk profile: **Low**

Control evolves alongside the system.

Level 5 Autonomous Control

Self-regulating systems with embedded control intelligence. Governance is integrated into system design, not layered on top. AI manages its own constraints with full transparency and traceability.

- Minimal human involvement strategic only
- Full transparency and traceability
- Controlled and optimised performance
- Risk profile: **Optimised**

AI systems operate with built-in governance and self-control.

Comparative View Across All Levels

The table below maps each dimension of maturity across all six levels, providing a structured reference for benchmarking and assessment. Use this to locate your current state and identify which dimensions lag behind overall maturity.

Dimension	L0	L1	L2	L3	L4	L5
Governance	None	Policy	Process	Enforced	Adaptive	Embedded
Decision Control	None	Limited	Partial	Strong	Dynamic	Autonomous
Human Role	None	Reactive	Selective	Structured	Strategic	Minimal
Observability	None	Basic	Structured	Advanced	Real-time	Full
Risk	Very High	High	Moderate	Controlled	Low	Optimised

Common Misclassifications and the Maturity Gap

Organisations consistently overestimate their maturity level. Three specific misclassifications account for the majority of assessment errors. Recognising these patterns is a prerequisite for accurate positioning.

Policy ≠ Level 2

Having documented policies does not mean control is defined. Policies without enforcement mechanisms reflect Level 1 awareness at best.

Monitoring ≠ Level 3

Observing system behaviour is not the same as enforcing control. Metrics without runtime guardrails do not constitute Level 3 maturity.

Automation ≠ Level 5

Autonomy without embedded control is not maturity it is risk. High automation at low governance is characteristic of Level 0, not Level 5.

> Most organisations operate at Level 1 or 2 while believing they are at Level 3 or higher. This gap creates **false confidence and hidden risk** the most dangerous combination in AI governance.

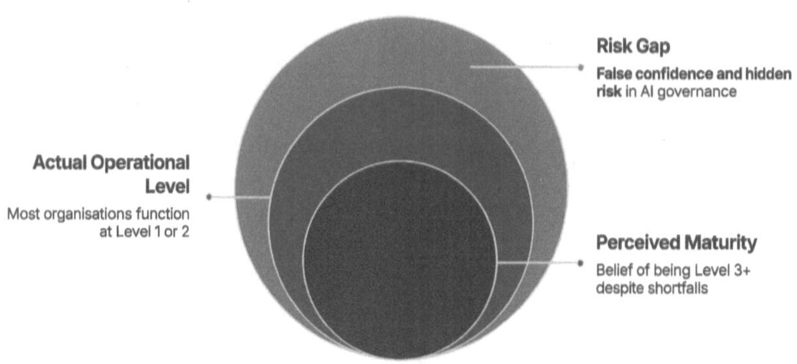

Identifying Your Level & Moving Forward

Accurate self-assessment requires asking the right diagnostic questions across four dimensions. The answers not the intentions indicate maturity level.

1 Control

Are decision boundaries defined and enforced? Are guardrails active at runtime not just documented in policy?

2 Visibility

Can decisions be traced and explained after the fact? Is there a complete audit trail for high-stakes outputs?

3 Intervention

Can the system stop, pause, or escalate decisions based on defined conditions automatically or via structured human review?

4 Adaptability

Does the system adjust to changing conditions, or do controls remain static regardless of context drift?

Maturity is not defined by what an organisation claims. It is defined by what its systems consistently do. **Your AI maturity is not your intention. It is your execution.**

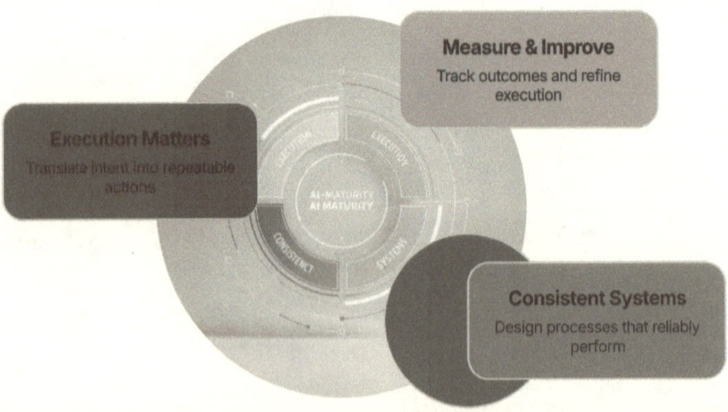

Characteristics of Each Maturity Level

Chapter 19

Diagnosing Your Organisation

Most organisations believe they understand their AI systems what models are deployed, which use cases are active, which metrics are improving. But ask a harder question: **"How controlled are these systems, end to end?"** The answer is often unclear. AI systems are distributed across teams, embedded in multiple processes, and evolving continuously. Control becomes fragmented, inconsistent, and difficult to assess. You cannot improve what you cannot diagnose. Before building control, organisations must first understand where they truly stand.

The Purpose of Diagnosis

Diagnosis is not an audit. It is not about compliance. It is about understanding the **actual behaviour** of AI systems in operation not their intended behaviour as documented, but what they genuinely do when running in production environments under real conditions.

A strong diagnosis provides the foundation for everything that follows: clarity on current maturity, identification of gaps, and a prioritised path to improvement. Without it, organisations are building controls on assumptions rather than evidence.

> ⓘ Diagnosis converts perceived control into measured control the essential shift for any mature AI governance programme.

Clarity

Understand current maturity across all dimensions

Identification

Surface gaps between policy intent and system reality

Prioritisation

Focus effort where risk and impact are highest

Roadmap

Define a clear path from current state to target state

Why Diagnosis Is Hard

Diagnosing AI control is structurally difficult. The same properties that make AI systems powerful their distribution, autonomy, and adaptability are exactly what makes them hard to assess.

Systems Are Distributed

AI exists across products, platforms, and business units. No single team has end-to-end visibility, creating blind spots at every organisational boundary.

Ownership Is Fragmented

Different teams manage data, models, decisions, and operations independently. Accountability gaps emerge between functions without anyone being responsible for the full control chain.

Visibility Is Partial

Organisations see metrics and outputs but not decision logic or control mechanisms. What looks controlled from the outside may be entirely unmanaged internally.

Assumptions Replace Evidence

Many conclusions are drawn from documentation and intent rather than actual system behaviour. The gap between what systems are *supposed* to do and what they *actually* do is often significant.

Five Dimensions of Diagnosis

A comprehensive diagnosis evaluates AI control across five interconnected dimensions. Each dimension probes a different layer of the control stack from policy intent through to operational adaptability.

1

Governance

Are policies defined, aligned with regulations, and actionable? **Key question:** Is intent clearly defined?

2

Decision Control

Are decision boundaries, thresholds, and escalation paths implemented? **Key question:** Are decisions controlled or unrestricted?

3

System Architecture

Are control points embedded and guardrails active? **Key question:** Is control designed into the system?

4

Observability

Are decisions logged and traceable with explanations available? **Key question:** Can the system be understood?

5

Adaptability

Does the system detect drift and evolve its controls? **Key question:** Can the system adjust to change?

Maturity Levels Across Dimensions

Each of the five dimensions can be evaluated across maturity levels from L0 (absent) through L5 (fully adaptive). The table below provides a diagnostic reference for assessing current state and identifying where to invest improvement effort.

Dimension	L0–L1	L2	L3	L4–L5
Governance	Absent / basic	Defined	Enforced	Adaptive
Decision Control	None	Partial	Strong	Dynamic
Architecture	Ad hoc	Structured	Embedded	Optimised
Observability	Minimal	Basic	Advanced	Full
Adaptability	None	Limited	Moderate	Continuous

> Most organisations discover they are at L1–L2 across multiple dimensions on first diagnosis. This is normal and exactly the kind of clarity diagnosis is designed to produce.

Diagnostic Methods

Effective diagnosis requires multiple complementary methods. No single approach provides the full picture organisations must triangulate across system data, process evidence, and human insight.

1

System Review

Analyse AI pipelines, decision flows, and embedded control points

2

Process Mapping

Trace how decisions move through systems, where controls exist, where gaps appear

3

Stakeholder Interviews

Engage engineering, product, risk, and operations for cross-functional insight

4

Scenario Testing

Simulate edge cases and high-risk conditions to test control robustness

Key Diagnostic Questions

Good diagnosis is question-driven. The following questions cut through documentation and surface the actual state of control. Use these as interview guides, self-assessment tools, or audit prompts across teams.

Control

Can the system stop itself? Can it escalate decisions? Are boundaries enforced at runtime?

Visibility

Can decisions be traced end to end? Are logs comprehensiv e and accessible?

Risk

What happens in edge cases? How are anomalies detected and handled when they occur?

Adaptation

How does the system respond to change? Are feedback loops validated and acting on signal?

Identifying and Prioritising Gaps

Four Common Gap Types

Policy–Execution Gap

Policies exist but systems do not enforce them. Intent is defined; operationalisation is absent.

Visibility Gap

Decisions cannot be traced. Logging is absent, incomplete, or inaccessible to those who need it.

Control Gap

No boundaries or guardrails constrain system behaviour. Decisions are effectively unrestricted.

Adaptation Gap

Systems do not detect or respond to drift. Feedback loops are absent or unvalidated.

Prioritisation Framework

Not all gaps are equal. Prioritise remediation based on four factors:

1 Risk Impact

Address high-risk systems first, regardless of ease of remediation

2 Decision Criticality

High-impact, irreversible decisions warrant priority investment in control

3 Scale

Systems affecting large populations carry proportionally greater organisational exposure

4 Feasibility

Balance quick wins that build momentum against longer-term structural changes

Avoiding Diagnostic Pitfalls

Diagnosis fails when organisations take shortcuts. The most common mistakes systematically produce false confidence leaving leaders believing control is stronger than it actually is.

Over-Reliance on Documentation

Assuming that policy equals control. Documents describe intent they do not enforce behaviour. Always test what systems actually do.

Narrow Scope

Evaluating only specific, visible systems while leaving shadow AI, embedded models, and vendor systems unexamined.

Ignoring Runtime Behaviour

Focusing only on design-time architecture. Systems behave differently in production diagnosis must include live operational evidence.

Lack of Cross-Functional Input

Missing the holistic view by excluding risk, operations, or legal. A single team's perspective will always produce an incomplete diagnosis.

From Diagnosis to Action

Diagnosis Must Lead Somewhere

Diagnosis is only valuable if it produces action. A completed diagnosis should result in four concrete outputs: a clear maturity level for each dimension, a documented gap list, a defined set of priorities, and a roadmap for improvement with owners and timelines.

The shift that diagnosis enables is fundamental moving organisations from **perceived control** to **measured control**. That shift is the prerequisite for everything in the chapters ahead.

> Control begins with awareness. But awareness must be grounded in reality not assumption. You cannot control your AI systems until you truly understand how they behave.

Build the Roadmap

Translate priorities into a sequenced improvement plan with owners and milestones

Define Priorities

Rank gaps by risk impact, decision criticality, scale, and feasibility

Identify the Gaps

Surface policy–execution, visibility, control, and adaptation gaps across all five dimensions

Establish Current State

Score maturity across governance, decision control, architecture, observability, and adaptability

Next: Once the current state is clear, the path forward begins. Chapter 20 explores *Moving Up the Curve The Transformation Path.*

Chapter 20

Moving Up the Curve

Most organisations recognise the need for better AI control. They define policies, introduce processes, and invest in tools yet progress remains slow. Moving from awareness to control is not a single initiative. It is a **systemic transformation**: a coordinated evolution across systems, processes, and decision-making that builds genuine, scalable control into the fabric of how AI operates.

From Diagnosis to Transformation

Understanding where you are matters but what matters more is how you move forward. Diagnosis reveals your current maturity level, existing gaps, and areas of risk. Transformation turns that clarity into direction, structure, and execution.

What Diagnosis Provides

- Current maturity level
- Existing capability gaps
- Areas of concentrated risk

What Transformation Provides

- Clear direction and intent
- Structured progression path
- Execution at scale

Without a structured approach, efforts remain fragmented, improvements are inconsistent, and control does not scale.

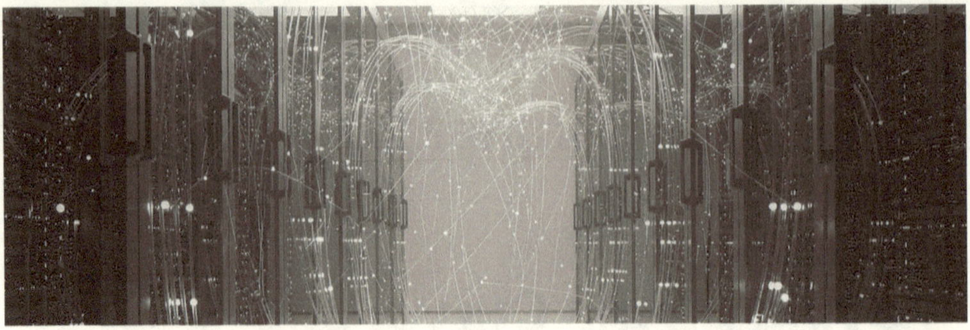

The Transformation Challenge

Moving up the maturity curve is complex. AI systems are deeply embedded in core operations, customer-facing processes, and critical infrastructure. Change requires coordinated effort and most organisations face significant structural headwinds.

AI Systems Are Embedded

Integrated into core operations, customer journeys, and critical infrastructure changes ripple across the entire stack.

Change Requires Coordination

Engineering, Product, Risk, and Operations must all align. Siloed action yields fragmented control.

Legacy Systems Exist

Older systems lack built-in control mechanisms and often require fundamental redesign rather than incremental patching.

Culture Must Shift

From a speed-first mindset to a control-aware mindset a change that requires leadership commitment, not just policy.

Transformation Principles

Successful transformation is not improvised. It follows a set of guiding principles that shape how organisations progress through each maturity stage ensuring control is built systematically rather than bolted on reactively.

Incremental Progression

Move step-by-step between maturity levels. Attempting to skip stages leads to brittle, unsustainable control.

Risk-Based Prioritisation

Focus resources on high-impact, high-risk systems first. Not every system demands immediate transformation.

System-Level Thinking

Address architecture holistically not just individual components. Control must be designed in, not added later.

Continuous Evolution

Adapt as systems and environments change. Maturity is a moving target, not a fixed destination.

The Five-Stage Maturity Progression

Transformation unfolds across five distinct stages from basic awareness through to fully autonomous control. Each stage has a clear objective, defined actions, and measurable outcomes. The most critical transition is from **Defined to Enforced**: the moment control moves from design into live execution.

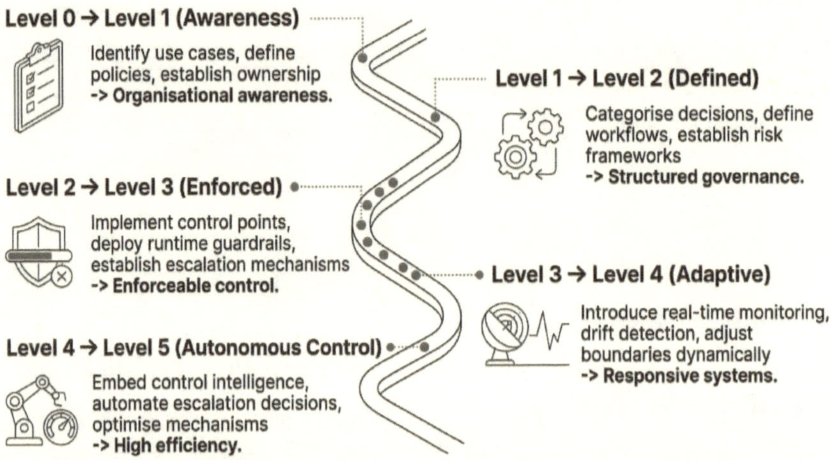

⚠ The transition from Level 2 (Defined) to Level 3 (Enforced) is the most critical this is where control moves from documentation to live execution. Most organisations stall here.

Key Transformation Levers

Across all stages, transformation requires coordinated progress across five interdependent levers. Neglecting any one of them creates gaps that undermine the others. True control only emerges when all five are advancing together.

Architecture

Embed control directly into system design not as an afterthought, but as a foundational requirement from the outset.

Processes

Align operational workflows with system behaviour. Approval paths, escalation routes, and review cycles must reflect AI risk realities.

Technology

Implement runtime guardrails, monitoring infrastructure, and drift detection tooling as core platform capabilities.

People

Define clear roles, responsibilities, and accountability structures. Control without ownership remains aspirational.

Governance

Ensure alignment with internal policies and external regulations. Governance is the connective tissue between all other levers.

Prioritisation, Quick Wins & Measuring Progress

Not all systems require immediate transformation. A pragmatic prioritisation strategy focuses effort where risk and impact are highest while delivering early wins that build organisational confidence and momentum.

Prioritisation Criteria

- **Impact** high-impact systems first
- **Risk Exposure** systems with elevated risk profiles
- **Scale** systems affecting large user bases
- **Regulatory Sensitivity** compliance-critical systems

Quick Wins

- Define decision boundaries
- Introduce basic guardrails
- Improve monitoring coverage

Long-Term Changes

- Redesign system architecture
- Implement dynamic control
- Build adaptive systems

Measuring Progress

- Reduction in uncontrolled decisions
- Increased decision visibility
- Improved incident response time
- Lower risk incident frequency

What gets measured gets managed. Define metrics before transformation begins.

Alignment, Pitfalls & the Road Ahead

Transformation without alignment fails. Leadership sets direction; Engineering implements systems; Risk defines controls; Operations manages execution. When these functions are not aligned, control remains fragmented regardless of the tools deployed.

Pitfall: Treating Control as Compliance

Focusing on documentation rather than live enforcement produces a governance theatre not genuine control.

Pitfall: Overengineering Early

Attempting Level 5 capabilities at Level 1 maturity wastes resources and undermines credibility. Progress incrementally.

Pitfall: Ignoring Legacy Systems

Leaving critical older systems uncontrolled creates dangerous blind spots, regardless of how mature newer systems become.

Pitfall: Lack of Ownership

Without clear accountability, control initiatives stall. Every control mechanism needs a named owner and defined mandate.

> AI systems will continue to grow in capability. The question is whether control grows with them. Transformation is not about adding control later it is about building systems where **control is intrinsic**.

ⓘ The next chapter explores: **Embedding Control in the AI Lifecycle** applying these principles in real enterprise environments.

Chapter 21

Embedding Control in the AI Lifecycle

Most organisations treat AI control as a checkpoint a review before deployment, an approval before release, an audit after execution. But AI systems do not operate at a single point in time. They evolve, adapt, and learn continuously. If control exists only at one stage, it quickly becomes irrelevant. **Control must not be a checkpoint. It must be a continuous property of the lifecycle.**

The AI Lifecycle

An AI system moves through a series of interconnected stages, each introducing decisions, risks, and opportunities for governance. Control must be present at every stage not bolted on at the end.

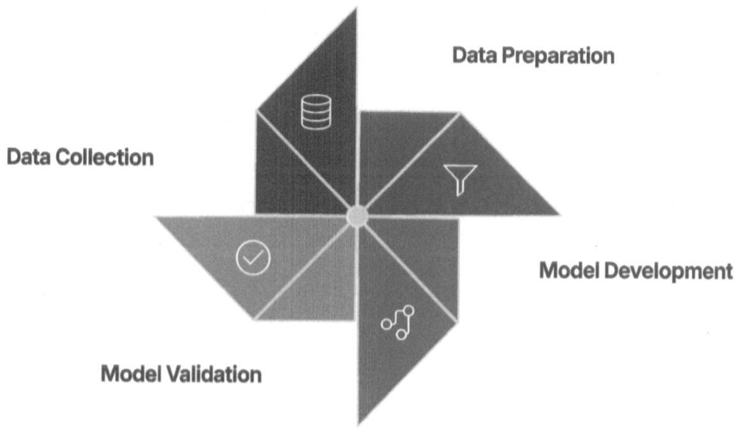

Each stage is a point of influence. Treating any one of them as outside the scope of governance creates gaps that compound over time, causing systems to drift from their intended purpose.

Why Lifecycle Control Matters

Without Lifecycle Integration

Fragmented Control

Governance exists in silos, disconnected from the systems it is meant to oversee.

Emergent Gaps

Handoffs between stages become blind spots where risk accumulates undetected.

Drift from Intent

Systems evolve away from their original objectives without anyone noticing.

With Lifecycle Control

Continuous Governance

Oversight is embedded into every stage, not applied retrospectively.

Aligned Decisions

Each decision point reinforces the system's intended objectives.

Proactive Risk Management

Risks are identified and mitigated before they propagate downstream.

Control Across Lifecycle Stages

Every stage of the AI lifecycle carries distinct risks. Each requires tailored control mechanisms designed to prevent those risks from compounding into larger failures.

Data Collection

Risks: Biased or incomplete datasets, data quality issues

Controls: Data validation rules, source verification, governance policies

Data Preparation

Risks: Feature engineering bias, data leakage, inconsistent transforms

Controls: Standardised pipelines, validation checks, version control

Model Development

Risks: Overfitting, misaligned objectives, lack of explainability

Controls: Evaluation criteria, multi-objective optimisation, interpretability

Model Validation

Risks: Limited test scenarios, ignored edge cases, overconfidence in performance

Controls: Scenario testing, stress testing, bias and fairness checks

Control in Deployment and Operations

The latter stages of the AI lifecycle where systems interact with the real world carry the highest operational risk. Controls here must be active, not passive.

🚀 Deployment

Risks: Incorrect configuration, incomplete monitoring, missing guardrails

Controls: Deployment checklists, control point validation, guardrail integration

Objective: Deploy with embedded control.

⚙️ Runtime Operation

Risks: Model drift, unexpected inputs, autonomous misalignment

Controls: Runtime guardrails, decision boundaries, kill switches

Objective: Maintain controlled execution.

📡 Monitoring & Feedback

Risks: Delayed detection, reinforcing incorrect behaviour, lack of visibility

Controls: Observability systems, feedback validation, anomaly detection

Objective: Detect and correct issues early.

🔄 Iteration & Update

Risks: Uncontrolled updates, regression issues, loss of alignment

Controls: Version management, controlled rollout, revalidation

Objective: Ensure safe system evolution.

Control Continuity & Integration

Control must flow unbroken across the entire lifecycle chain. Any gap in continuity creates compounding risk. Embedding control also requires deep integration with the engineering practices that govern how AI systems are built and operated.

The Continuity Chain

1. Data
2. Model
3. Decision
4. Action
5. Feedback

End-to-end governance requires that no handoff between these stages is left unmonitored. Where continuity breaks, control weakens and risk increases.

Integration Requirements

DevOps

Automated checks embedded in software delivery pipelines

MLOps

Continuous validation integrated into model lifecycle management

Shift-Left: Embedding Control Early

> Control introduced at the design stage costs a fraction of control retrofitted after deployment.

The shift-left principle demands that governance is woven into AI systems from the earliest stages of design and development not applied as a final gate before release. Early integration fundamentally changes the risk profile of a system.

Checkpoint Thinking

Reactive

Control applied after problems have already emerged

Costly

Rework and remediation consume disproportionate resources

Fragile

Single-point failures undermine the entire governance model

Lifecycle Thinking

Proactive

Risks are designed out before they can materialise

Efficient

Prevention is embedded at the lowest-cost intervention point

Resilient

Governance persists through change, updates, and evolution

Ownership, Design Principles & Common Gaps

Effective lifecycle control requires cross-functional alignment. No single team owns the full lifecycle and gaps in accountability are among the most common sources of governance failure.

Cross-Functional Ownership

Data Teams

Input quality and representativenes s

Engineering

System integrity and pipeline control

Product

Decision alignment with business objectives

Risk & Governance

Enterprise accountability and compliance

Common Governance Gaps

- ⚠ Control only at deployment no runtime enforcement
- ⚠ Weak feedback validation reinforces incorrect behaviour
- ⚠ Uncontrolled updates introduce regression and alignment risk
- ⚠ Fragmented ownership no clear accountability chain

Core Design Principles

End-to-End Integration	Automation
Control must span all lifecycle stages without exception	Embed control into pipelines to ensure consistent application
Consistency	**Adaptability**
Standardise mechanisms across teams and systems	Controls must evolve as systems change and mature

> AI systems are not static products. They are evolving systems. Control must evolve with them at every stage, continuously, and deliberately.

Chapter 22

Governance Operating Model

Policies are written. Frameworks are defined. Committees are formed. Yet when something goes wrong, one question surfaces immediately: **"Who owns this?"** This chapter examines why governance requires more than rules it demands a clear operating model that defines ownership, accountability, and decision rights across every function that touches an AI system.

The Core Problem: Unclear Ownership

Most organisations agree that AI must be governed. The frameworks exist. The committees meet. But governance fails not because rules are missing it fails because ownership is unclear. Without a defined operating model, control becomes fragmented, responsibility diffuses across teams, and systems operate without unified oversight.

Ownership

Who owns the AI system, the decisions it makes, and the risk it creates?

Accountability

Who is answerable when a system behaves unexpectedly or causes harm?

Decision Rights

Who can approve, override, or halt AI operations when required?

> Governance fails not because rules are missing but because ownership is unclear.

What Is a Governance Operating Model?

Definition

A governance operating model defines how control is implemented, managed, and enforced across an organisation. It is the structural backbone that turns policy into practice.

It answers the questions that frameworks alone cannot: who defines policies, who enforces them, who monitors systems, and who intervenes when needed.

Why It Is Necessary

AI systems span multiple functions Data, Engineering, Product, Risk, and Operations. Each function owns a part of the system, holds different priorities, and uses different tools.

Without a unified model, control becomes inconsistent and incomplete. A governance operating model closes this gap by connecting people, process, and system architecture into a coherent whole.

Core Components of the Operating Model

An effective governance operating model is built from five interdependent components. Each one addresses a distinct failure point and together they form a complete control capability.

1 **Ownership Structure**

Define who owns AI systems, decisions, and risk. Clear ownership ensures accountability, faster response, and better cross-functional alignment.

2 **Decision Rights**

Define who can approve decisions, override system outputs, or stop operations entirely. Without this, escalation fails and control mechanisms weaken.

3 **Roles and Responsibilities**

Every function Leadership, Engineering, Product, Risk, Operations, and Data must have explicitly defined contributions to governance control.

4 **Governance Processes**

Approval workflows, escalation mechanisms, and incident response procedures ensure consistency, repeatability, and clear accountability across the organisation.

5 **Control Integration**

Policies must translate into actual system behaviour. Control mechanisms must be embedded not bolted on after deployment.

Roles and Responsibilities Across Functions

Governance is not the responsibility of a single team. Every function plays a defined role in maintaining control. The table below maps each function to its core governance obligations.

Function	Primary Role	Key Responsibilities
Leadership (Board/CXO)	Strategic direction	Set risk appetite, ensure compliance, define governance mandate
Engineering	Control infrastructure	Build guardrails, implement controls, maintain system integrity
Product	Use case alignment	Define use cases, align AI decisions with business objectives
Risk & Compliance	Policy and monitoring	Define policies, monitor adherence, assess ongoing risk exposure
Operations	Runtime continuity	Monitor system behaviour, handle escalations, ensure continuity
Data Teams	Data governance	Ensure data quality, manage data governance standards

ⓘ Each role contributes to control. No single function can sustain governance in isolation.

Centralised vs. Distributed Governance

Organisations must make a deliberate structural choice about how governance authority is distributed. Each model carries distinct trade-offs in speed, consistency, and scalability.

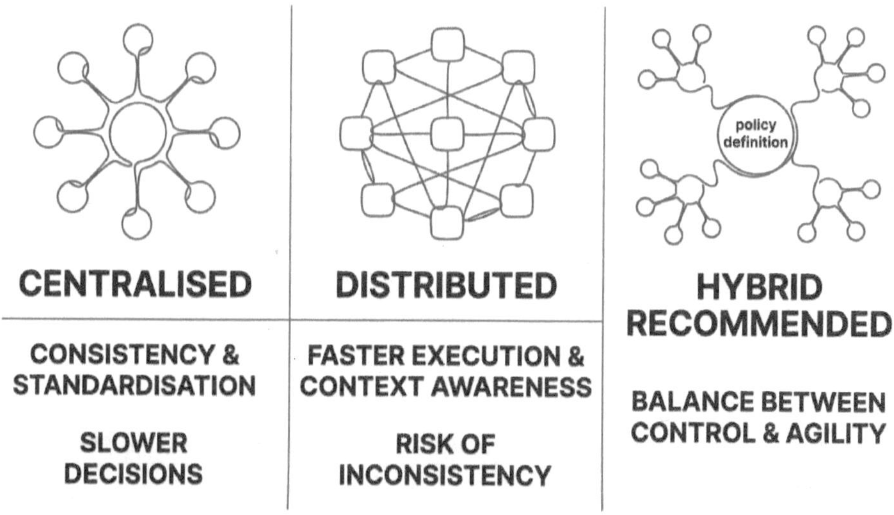

The **Hybrid Model** is recommended: central policy definition combined with distributed enforcement delivers the balance between control and agility that large-scale AI programmes require.

The Role of AI Governance Committees

What Committees Do

Governance committees serve a legitimate and important function. They review use cases, approve deployments, and provide structured oversight of AI programmes. They bring cross-functional perspective and create a formal review record.

For strategic decisions and periodic audits, committees are a necessary mechanism not an optional one.

What Committees Cannot Do

Committees operate periodically. They do not control runtime behaviour. They cannot intervene in real time when a model drifts, an escalation fires, or a threshold is breached.

Committees support governance they do not enforce it. The operating model must embed control directly into systems, not rely on scheduled meetings to maintain it.

> Governance must be executed not just defined. Embedding control into architecture is what makes it real.

Embedding Governance into Systems

The operating model must connect to active control points guardrails, escalation mechanisms, and monitoring infrastructure. This is how governance becomes operational rather than aspirational.

Control Points

Embed policy logic directly into system pipelines. Controls must trigger automatically, not depend on human review cycles.

Guardrails

Define hard and soft boundaries for system behaviour. Guardrails constrain outputs before they reach downstream systems or users.

Escalation Mechanisms

Define who receives escalations, who makes decisions, and who acts on outcomes. Without this clarity, delays compound and risk increases.

Accountability Framework

Accountability must be explicit, documented, and enforced. Three distinct ownership roles form the accountability backbone of any governance operating model.

System Owner

Responsible for the **behaviour** of the AI system in production. Accountable for technical performance, reliability, and adherence to guardrails. The first point of contact when system behaviour is questioned.

Decision Owner

Accountable for the **outcomes** of decisions made by or with AI systems. Responsible for ensuring decision logic aligns with policy, business intent, and regulatory requirements.

Risk Owner

Accountable for **exposure** the aggregate risk profile of AI systems across the organisation. Responsible for risk assessment, escalation thresholds, and mitigation strategy.

⚠ Without explicit accountability assignment, all three roles default to no one and governance collapses at the point of failure.

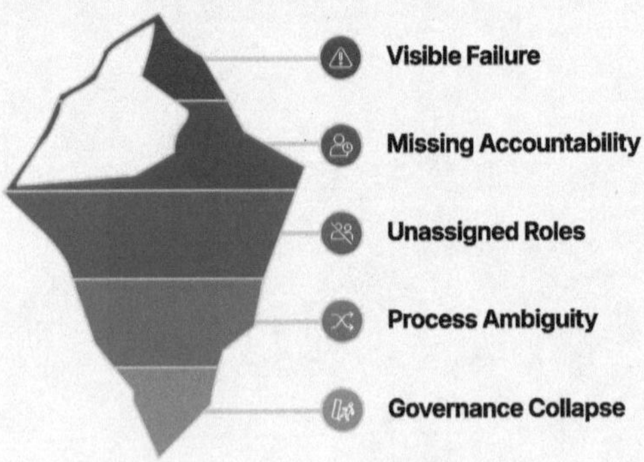

Common Failure Patterns

Understanding where governance operating models break down is as important as understanding how to build them. These four patterns account for the majority of governance failures in practice.

Diffused Ownership

Multiple teams share nominal ownership with no team holding actual accountability. When an incident occurs, responsibility is contested rather than acted upon.

Governance as Compliance

Governance is reduced to documentation and audit readiness. Policies exist on paper but are not connected to system behaviour or runtime controls.

Lack of Integration

Governance processes operate separately from engineering systems. Control mechanisms are not embedded they are applied after the fact, if at all.

Over-Centralisation

A central team holds all decision authority, creating bottlenecks that slow down deployment and reduce teams' ability to respond quickly to local risk signals.

Design Principles for a Robust Operating Model

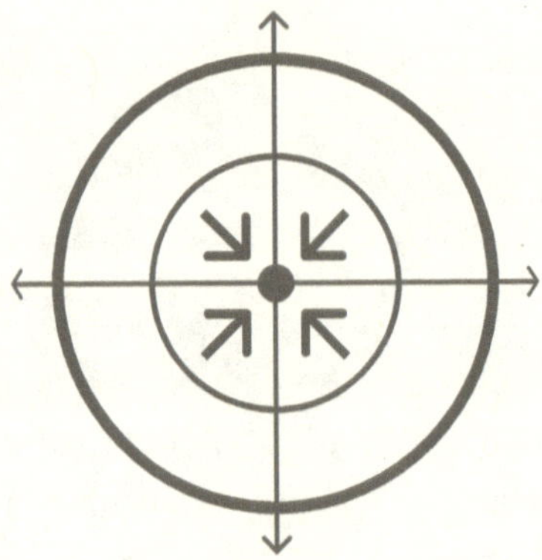

These four principles are not aspirational they are structural requirements. An operating model that lacks clarity will produce ambiguity under pressure. One that is not integrated with system architecture will be bypassed in practice. Governance built to these principles becomes a durable capability, not a periodic exercise.

Measuring Governance Effectiveness

Governance maturity must be measured, not assumed. Organisations require concrete metrics that signal whether the operating model is functioning as designed and where it is beginning to degrade.

4

Core Metric Categories

Incident response, escalation volume, control violations, and system reliability

- **Response time to incidents** measures speed of the escalation chain
- **Number of escalations** indicates where decision rights are unclear
- **Control violations** flags gaps between policy and system behaviour
- **System reliability** tracks operational continuity under governance

ⓘ These metrics indicate the **strength of governance** not merely its existence. An organisation that cannot measure governance effectiveness cannot improve it.

Establish baselines early. Track trends over time. Use degradation in metrics as an early warning signal, not a post-incident finding.

From Governance to Control Capability

The ultimate objective of the governance operating model is transformation converting governance from a set of policies and committees into a **structured, repeatable, and scalable organisational capability**.

Defined Rules

Policies, frameworks, and documented standards in place

Assigned Ownership

Clear accountability for systems, decisions, and risk exposure

Integrated Controls

Governance embedded in system architecture and runtime behaviour

Scalable Capability

A repeatable function that grows with the organisation's AI footprint

Key Takeaways

Chapter 22 establishes the governance operating model as the structural foundation for AI control. The following principles define what effective governance looks like in practice.

→ **A clear operating model is non-negotiable**

Governance without a defined operating model is policy without enforcement it exists on paper but not in practice.

→ **Control depends on ownership, decision rights, and defined roles**

These three elements form the accountability backbone. Without all three, governance is structurally incomplete.

→ **Hybrid governance models balance control and agility**

Centralised policy with distributed enforcement is the recommended structure for organisations operating at scale.

→ **Governance must be integrated with system architecture**

Policies that are not embedded in systems are not enforced. Integration is what separates governance from compliance theatre.

→ **Governance is a capability not just a framework**

The end state is a structured, repeatable, and measurable function not a document or a committee.

Chapter 23

Managing AI Risk

Every organisation deploying AI is managing risk whether it realises it or not. The difference lies not in whether risk exists, but in how deliberately it is addressed. AI systems introduce a new class of risk: continuous, scalable, and embedded within every decision the system makes. Risk is no longer episodic. It is systemic.

What Is AI Risk?

AI risk is the potential for AI-driven decisions to produce unintended, harmful, or misaligned outcomes. Unlike traditional operational risk confined to infrastructure, transactions, or isolated events AI risk is embedded in every decision a system makes. It arises from the full stack of AI development and deployment.

Data

Bias, gaps, and quality issues at the point of ingestion

Models

Misalignment, overfitting, and drift over time

Decisions

Incorrect outputs and misclassified outcomes at scale

System Behaviour

Emergent patterns that compound risk across the lifecycle

⚠ AI risk is not confined to infrastructure or isolated events it is embedded in every decision the system makes.

Types of AI Risk

AI risk spans multiple dimensions, each requiring distinct identification, assessment, and mitigation strategies. Understanding the taxonomy is the foundation for deliberate risk management.

1. **Decision Risk**

   Incorrect decisions, misclassification, and misaligned outputs that affect users or business processes

2. **Operational Risk**

   System failure, performance degradation, and process disruption at runtime

3. **Model Risk**

   Bias, drift, and overfitting that erode model accuracy and fairness over time

4. **Compliance Risk**

   Regulatory violations and lack of transparency in decision logic

5. **Reputational Risk**

   Loss of trust and brand damage resulting from harmful AI outcomes

6. **Strategic Risk**

   Misalignment with business goals and long-term organisational impact

The Nature of AI Risk

AI risk differs fundamentally from traditional risk. Four properties make it uniquely challenging and uniquely dangerous when left unmanaged.

Scale

A single model issue can propagate across millions of decisions simultaneously far beyond the reach of any traditional control

Speed

Decisions occur in real time, compressing the window for human intervention to near zero

Opacity

Decision logic may not be fully visible, making root cause analysis difficult and accountability elusive

Adaptability

Systems evolve over time, meaning the risk profile of a deployed model changes continuously without explicit redeployment

> AI risk is dynamic and continuous not a one-time assessment at deployment, but an ongoing responsibility throughout the system's operational life.

Risk vs Uncertainty & the Risk Lifecycle

Risk vs Uncertainty

Risk is known and measurable it can be modelled, quantified, and planned for.

Uncertainty is unknown and unpredictable it lies beyond the reach of historical data and probability models.

AI systems operate in both domains simultaneously. Effective governance must handle known risks while building organisational capacity to absorb uncertainty.

The AI Risk Lifecycle

Risk is not confined to a single stage it must be actively managed at every phase of an AI system's lifecycle.

→ **Data**

Bias and quality issues enter at the point of ingestion

→ **Model**

Misalignment and drift accumulate during training and deployment

→ **Decision**

Incorrect outputs surface at inference time

→ **Action → Feedback**

Impact propagates to users and systems; errors may be reinforced through feedback loops

Risk Identification, Assessment & Prioritisation

The first step in deliberate risk management is surfacing risks before they materialise. Identification is followed immediately by structured assessment to prioritise action.

Identification Methods

- **System analysis** mapping decision flows and control gaps
- **Scenario testing** simulating adverse conditions and edge cases
- **Historical data review** examining past incidents and near-misses
- **Stakeholder input** gathering frontline and domain knowledge

Risk Assessment Matrix

Impact / Likelihood	Low	Medium	High
Low Impact	Low	Low	Medium
Medium Impact	Low	Medium	High
High Impact	Medium	High	Critical

This matrix helps prioritise mitigation effort against the risks that matter most.

Risk Mitigation & Control

Once risks are identified and assessed, mitigation reduces them through a layered set of mechanisms. No single control is sufficient effective risk management requires defence in depth.

Control Mechanisms

Guardrails and decision boundaries that constrain system behaviour within acceptable limits

Monitoring

Continuous anomaly detection and performance tracking to surface emerging issues in real time

Escalation

Structured pathways for human intervention when automated controls are insufficient

Redundancy

Backup systems and failover mechanisms that maintain continuity during disruption

Testing

Scenario and stress testing that validates system behaviour under adverse and edge-case conditions

Each risk must have a clear owner with defined responsibility. Without ownership, risks remain unmanaged regardless of how well they are identified.

Dynamic Risk Management: From Monitoring to Engineering

AI risk is not static. It demands continuous monitoring, real-time adjustments, and adaptive controls integrated directly with the system's control points, guardrails, and escalation mechanisms. Risk reporting must provide visibility, communication, and transparency covering risk levels, incidents, and mitigation actions.

Common Pitfalls to Avoid

Treating AI risk as traditional risk ignoring scale and speed

Reactive approach addressing issues only after impact has occurred

Lack of visibility limited observability into model behaviour

No ownership diffused accountability that leaves risks unmanaged

Key Takeaways

01

AI risk is **continuous and systemic** not episodic

02

It spans **six dimensions**: decision, operational, model, compliance, reputational, and strategic

03

Risk must be **identified, assessed, and mitigated** at every lifecycle stage

04

Control mechanisms are **central** not supplementary to risk management

05

The goal is **risk engineering**: building systems that inherently reduce risk

> The strength of an organisation is not in avoiding risk but in managing it deliberately, continuously, and intelligently. AI systems create value through decisions. But every decision carries risk.

Chapter 24

Third-Party AI Control

Most organisations believe they control their AI systems. They design models, pipelines, and control mechanisms yet a significant portion of AI capability now originates *outside* the organisation. This chapter confronts an uncomfortable reality: when you integrate rather than build, control becomes delegated, not direct. The central question follows: **How do you control what you do not fully own?**

The Rise of External AI Dependencies

Modern AI ecosystems are built on a foundation of third-party components large language models, fraud detection services, recommendation engines, and analytics platforms. These dependencies accelerate development, reduce cost, and enable rapid deployment. But they also introduce risks that organisations are only beginning to reckon with.

Accelerate Reduce time-to-deployment for AI capabilities across the enterprise	**Reduce Cost** Avoid the overhead of building and maintaining models from scratch
Enable Scale Access enterprise-grade AI without equivalent internal infrastructure	**Introduce Risk** Opaque logic, limited visibility, and reduced control over outcomes

⚠ The shift from **building** to **integrating** AI systems marks a fundamental transition from direct control to delegated control.

The Control Gap

When organisations deploy external AI, a structural gap emerges between who holds *responsibility* and who holds *control*. Responsibility remains firmly internal but the logic, behaviour, and updates of the model reside with the vendor.

Aspect	Internal AI	Third-Party AI
Model Visibility	High	Limited
Control over Logic	Full	Partial
Ability to Modify	High	Restricted
Responsibility	Clear	Shared

> **Responsibility remains internal but control is external.** This is the defining tension of third-party AI governance.

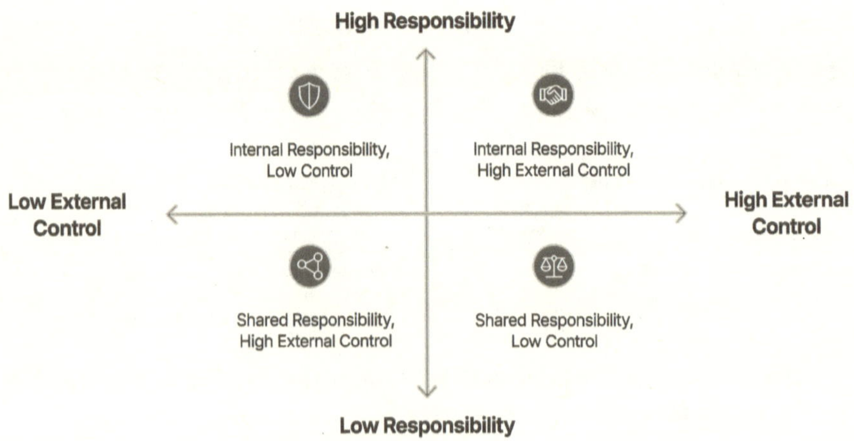

Types of Third-Party AI Risk

Third-party AI introduces a distinct risk profile. Unlike internal systems, these risks are compounded by limited visibility and vendor dependency making proactive identification essential.

Opaque Decision-Making

Limited visibility into model logic; black-box behaviour makes explainability and audit difficult.

Data Risk

Sensitive data shared externally creates exposure to misuse, leakage, or non-compliant handling.

Model Behaviour Risk

Unexpected outputs or misaligned objectives can propagate harm before detection.

Dependency Risk

Reliance on vendor availability means service disruptions directly impact operational continuity.

Compliance Risk

Vendors may not meet evolving regulatory requirements, yet the organisation remains liable.

Update Risk

Vendors may alter model behaviour without notice, changing outputs in production systems.

The Illusion of Outsourced Responsibility

The Assumption

"If the model is provided by a vendor, the risk is theirs."

This belief is pervasive and dangerously incorrect.

The Reality

Regardless of where the model resides, the **organisation owns the decision, the outcome, and the impact.** Regulators, customers, and courts do not distinguish between internal and external AI when assigning accountability.

Technology can be outsourced. **Accountability cannot.**

Third-party AI should be treated as **uncontrolled components within a controlled system.** This means control must exist *around* the component not within it.

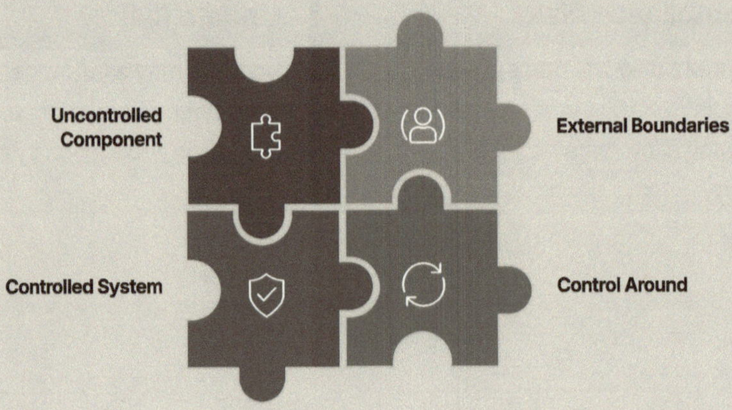

Control Strategies for Third-Party AI

Because organisations cannot govern what happens *inside* an external model, control must be applied at the boundaries through structured strategies that wrap, validate, and constrain third-party behaviour.

Input Control

Validate all data before sending to external systems. Prevent invalid inputs and sensitive data exposure at the source.

Output Control

Validate outputs before use. Block incorrect decisions or unexpected actions from propagating into downstream processes.

Boundary Enforcement

Define precisely where third-party AI may operate. Limit scope of influence to contain risk to specific, monitored contexts.

Monitoring & Logging

Track all interactions with external systems. Maintain visibility and traceability for audit, compliance, and incident response.

Fallback Mechanisms

Define alternatives if the vendor fails or produces unreliable outputs. Ensure operational continuity under degraded conditions.

Escalation Controls

Route high-risk outputs to human review. Manage uncertainty by inserting human judgement at critical decision points.

Vendor Evaluation & Contractual Controls

Governance of third-party AI begins before deployment. Rigorous vendor evaluation and contractually binding obligations are foundational not optional.

Vendor Evaluation Criteria

01

Transparency

Can decision logic be explained and audited?

02

Control Options

Can thresholds and behaviour be configured?

03

Compliance

Does the vendor meet applicable regulatory requirements?

04

Reliability

What are the uptime guarantees and stability commitments?

05

Update Policies

How are model changes communicated and managed?

Contract Must Define

Data Usage

Permitted uses, retention, and deletion of shared data

Liability

Clear allocation of accountability for harmful outcomes

Performance

SLAs, accuracy expectations, and breach remedies

Compliance

Obligations to meet regulatory standards, with audit rights

From Integration to Governance

The maturity journey for third-party AI does not end at integration. Organisations must evolve from merely consuming external AI services to actively governing the ecosystems in which those services operate.

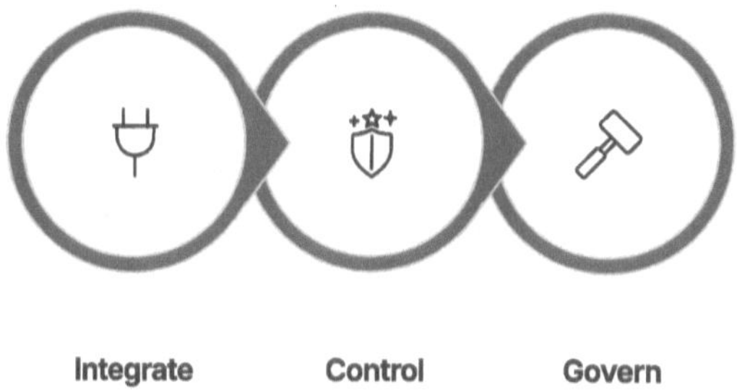

Each stage demands greater organisational capability moving from technical adoption through operational control to strategic governance. The next section applies these principles to real-world industry contexts, beginning with Telecom and BFSI.

Key Takeaway 1

Third-party AI introduces unique control challenges opaque behaviour, data exposure, and dependency risk.

Key Takeaway 2

Organisations retain full accountability for outcomes, regardless of where the model resides.

Key Takeaway 3

Control must be applied *around* external components through validation, monitoring, and escalation.

Key Takeaway 4

Vendor evaluation and contractual obligations are governance prerequisites, not afterthoughts.

> You may not control how external AI works **but you must control how it is used.**

Chapter 25

Telecom: Decision-Driven Networks

For decades, telecom has been defined by one core function: move data efficiently. That paradigm is ending. With the rise of AI-native architectures, networks are undergoing a fundamental shift from connectivity infrastructure to **decision infrastructure.** This chapter examines how telecom networks are evolving into autonomous, continuously deciding systems, and what control frameworks are required to govern them.

The Old Paradigm Is Ending

Traditional telecom success was measured in coverage, capacity, latency, and throughput. Networks were engineered as deterministic, rule-driven, human-controlled systems. That model served the industry well until AI-native architectures changed what a network could be.

The Old Measure of Success

- Coverage and capacity
- Latency and throughput
- Deterministic behaviour
- Rule-driven operations
- Human-controlled systems

The Emerging Reality

Networks are no longer just transporting data. They are:

- Interpreting context in real time
- Making autonomous decisions
- Executing actions at scale
- Continuously adapting to conditions

This transforms telecom into **a system that decides** continuously, autonomously, and at scale.

From Static Networks to Adaptive Systems

The architectural shift between traditional and AI-native networks is not incremental it is categorical. Where traditional networks reacted, AI-native networks anticipate. Where manual configuration was required, autonomous decision-making now operates.

Traditional Network	AI-Native Network
• Predefined rules	• Learns from data
• Manual intervention	• Autonomous operation
• Reactive to events	• Predictive by design
• Configuration-driven	• Decision-driven
• Static architecture	• Adaptive architecture

Modern networks already exhibit early forms of this decision-making: traffic routing adjustments, dynamic spectrum allocation, energy optimisation, and self-healing fault detection all increasingly driven by machine learning and closed-loop control systems.

Where Decisions Are Being Made

AI-driven decisions do not occur at a single point they are distributed continuously across every layer of the network stack.

1

Radio Access Network (RAN)

- Dynamic beamforming
- Spectrum allocation
- Interference management

2

Core Network

- Traffic steering
- Network slicing decisions
- Session management

3

Transport Network

- Routing optimisation
- Congestion management

4

Operations (OSS/BSS)

- Fault prediction
- Resource allocation
- Customer experience optimisation

ⓘ Across all layers, decisions are continuous and distributed making centralised human oversight structurally insufficient without proper governance frameworks.

The Control Challenge

As networks become decision-driven, human oversight reduces, automation increases, and system complexity grows. This combination introduces risks that traditional network engineering was never designed to address.

Uncontrolled Optimisation

Networks optimise relentlessly for efficiency metrics, potentially ignoring service quality, fairness, or operator intent.

Cascading Failures

Decisions at one network layer propagate errors across others. A localised anomaly can become a systemic outage.

Reduced Visibility

Complex AI decisions become difficult to trace, audit, or explain eroding operator confidence and regulatory compliance.

Real-Time Constraints

Decisions occur in milliseconds. Human intervention windows are vanishingly small, requiring pre-emptive control mechanisms.

⚠ Telecom networks are national infrastructure and business-critical systems. Failures carry service, financial, and regulatory consequences. **Control is not optional it is foundational.**

Applying the AI Control Framework

Governing decision-driven networks requires a structured, layered control framework applied consistently across the entire operation. Each layer addresses a distinct dimension of risk and oversight.

1

Policy Layer

Define service quality standards, fair usage policies, and regulatory compliance requirements.

2

Process Layer

Establish decision workflows, escalation procedures, and risk management processes.

3

Enforcement Layer

Implement decision boundaries, runtime guardrails, and control points across all network layers.

4

Interface Layer

Enable network visibility, operator intervention capabilities, and explainability of AI decisions.

Decision Boundaries in Practice

- Limit spectrum reallocation beyond defined thresholds
- Restrict traffic rerouting under critical conditions
- Escalate high-impact network changes to human operators

Runtime Guardrails & Kill Switches

- Confidence thresholds for autonomous AI decisions
- Rate limits on the pace of network changes
- Anomaly detection triggering automatic rollback
- Kill switches to disable optimisation and revert to predefined configurations

The Human Role in Decision-Driven Networks

Operators do not disappear in an AI-native network their role transforms fundamentally. The shift is from manual configuration to strategic governance, from execution to oversight.

From: Manual Configuration

Engineers configuring individual parameters, reacting to events, and managing the network rule by rule.

To: System Oversight

Operators setting policy boundaries, handling exceptions, and maintaining strategic control over autonomous systems.

Observability becomes the critical enabler of this shift. Operators must maintain end-to-end visibility, real-time monitoring, and full traceability of AI decisions not to approve every action, but to retain meaningful control when it matters most. Without observability, the human role in the loop is nominal rather than substantive.

> The goal is not to slow automation it is to ensure that automation operates within boundaries that humans define, monitor, and can override.

Towards the Decision Economy

This transformation is not merely operational it is strategic. Telecom operators must redefine their identity from infrastructure providers to **decision platforms**. The shift unlocks new value models: intelligent context-aware connectivity, AI-driven enterprise network optimisation, and **Decision-as-a-Service** revenue streams.

Intelligent Services

Context-aware connectivity that adapts to user behaviour, application demands, and environmental conditions in real time.

Enterprise Solutions

AI-driven network optimisation delivered as managed services, creating differentiated enterprise offerings.

New Revenue Models

Decision-as-a-Service: monetising the network's intelligence itself, not just its capacity.

> For decades, telecom moved information. Now, it is beginning to move decisions. The operators who succeed will not just connect the world they will control how it decides.

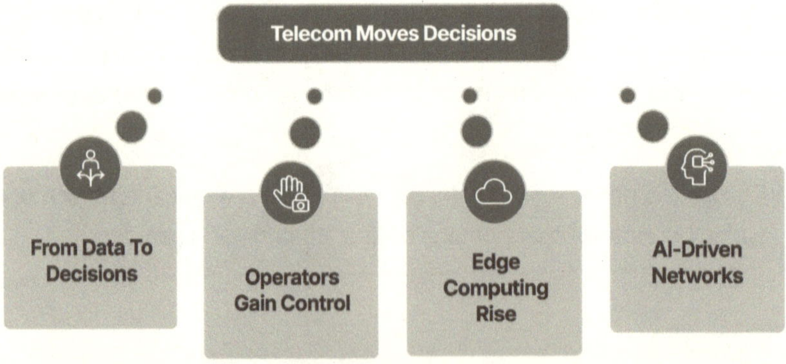

Chapter 26

BFSI: Regulated AI Systems

In most industries, AI adoption is driven by efficiency, scale, and innovation. In banking, financial services, and insurance (BFSI), there is an additional and overriding force: **regulation.** Every AI decision in BFSI carries financial implications, legal consequences, and customer trust impact. This chapter examines why that fundamentally changes how AI must be designed, deployed, and controlled.

Why BFSI Is Different

AI systems in BFSI are not merely optimisation engines. They are **regulated decision systems** operating under constraint, not freedom. Four forces distinguish BFSI from every other sector.

High Decision Impact

Decisions directly affect financial access, customer livelihood, and institutional risk making errors costly at every level.

Regulatory Oversight

Strong compliance requirements and audit obligations govern every system, process, and output produced by AI.

Accountability Requirements

Decisions must be explainable, traceable, and attributed to clear lines of responsibility within the organisation.

Low Tolerance for Error

Even small errors can trigger financial loss, legal consequences, and lasting reputational damage.

⚠ AI in BFSI operates under constraint — not freedom. This is the defining characteristic that shapes every design and governance decision.

AI Is Already Deeply Embedded in BFSI

From credit decisions to fraud detection, AI systems are already operating at scale across the full breadth of financial services making real-time decisions that directly affect financial outcomes.

Credit Scoring

Automated assessment of borrower risk and creditworthiness at scale.

Fraud Detection

Real-time identification and flagging of suspicious transactions.

Risk Assessment

Portfolio-level and individual risk quantification across products.

KYC Onboarding

Customer identity verification and compliance screening at intake.

Claims Processing

Automated assessment and routing of insurance claims submissions.

Algorithmic Trading

High-frequency, model-driven execution of market positions.

Core Challenges of AI in BFSI

The BFSI environment creates four structural tensions that AI governance must resolve. These are not abstract concerns they manifest daily in system design, model selection, and operational decisions.

Explainability vs. Performance

High-performing models are often complex and difficult to explain. Regulations require transparent decision-making creating a direct tension with model sophistication.

Bias and Fairness

AI decisions must avoid discrimination and unfair outcomes across protected characteristics a requirement that demands active monitoring and remediation.

Real-Time Decisions with Oversight

Systems must act quickly whilst remaining controlled balancing the speed of automation with the safeguards of human governance.

Regulatory Compliance

Systems must align with both local and global regulations, satisfying audit requirements across multiple jurisdictions simultaneously.

Applying the AI Control Framework to BFSI

In BFSI, control is not optional it is mandated. Organisations must demonstrate how decisions are made, how risks are managed, and how systems are governed. The AI Control Framework provides a structured four-layer response to this imperative.

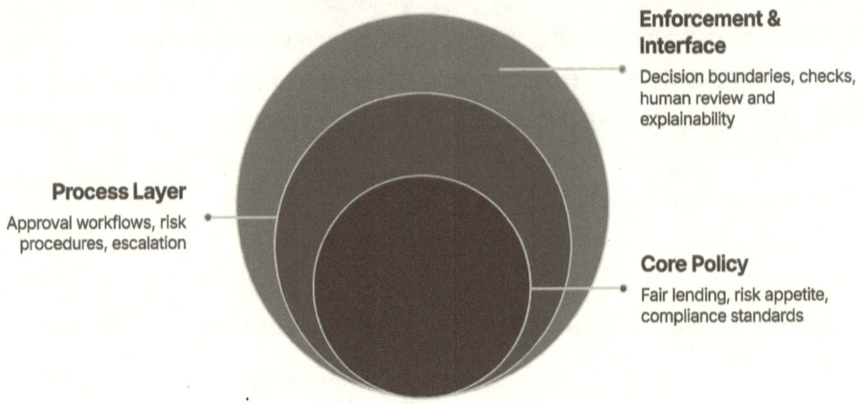

Each layer builds upon the last from defining organisational intent at the policy level, through to enabling human accountability at the interface. Together they form a complete governance architecture for regulated AI.

Decision Boundaries & Runtime Guardrails

Decision Boundaries

Hard limits that determine when AI operates autonomously and when human review is required.

- Credit approvals above threshold require human review
- High-risk transactions trigger automatic escalation
- Claims above a set value require validation before processing

Runtime Guardrails

Live controls that ensure compliance and controlled decision-making throughout system operation.

- Confidence thresholds for automated approvals
- Fraud risk scoring limits and alert bands
- Rate limits on transaction volumes and velocities

ⓘ Together, decision boundaries and runtime guardrails form the enforcement backbone of BFSI AI ensuring no decision escapes the bounds of policy and regulation.

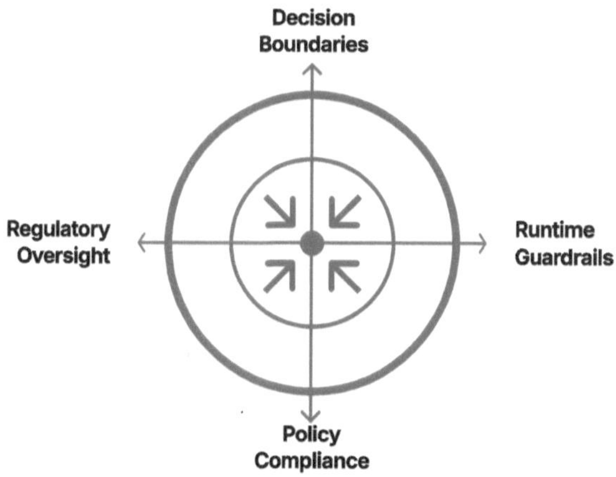

Human-in-the-Loop & Observability

Unlike many industries where automation is progressively replacing human review, BFSI demands ongoing human-in-the-loop (HITL) participation particularly for high-stakes, ambiguous, or regulatory-sensitive scenarios. Alongside HITL, full observability is a non-negotiable audit requirement.

Human-in-the-Loop

Required for high-value decisions, ambiguous cases, and any scenario with regulatory sensitivity. HITL is not a fallback it is by design.

Complete Traceability

Every decision must generate detailed, reproducible logs. Audits must be able to answer: why was this decided, what data was used, and what rules applied?

Continuous Observability

Systems must be monitored in real time for drift, bias, and performance degradation with alerts triggering review before compliance is breached.

Failure Scenarios in BFSI

AI failures in BFSI are not abstract risk events. Each carries a direct triple impact: financial loss, legal consequences, and reputational damage. Understanding failure modes is essential to designing systems that prevent them.

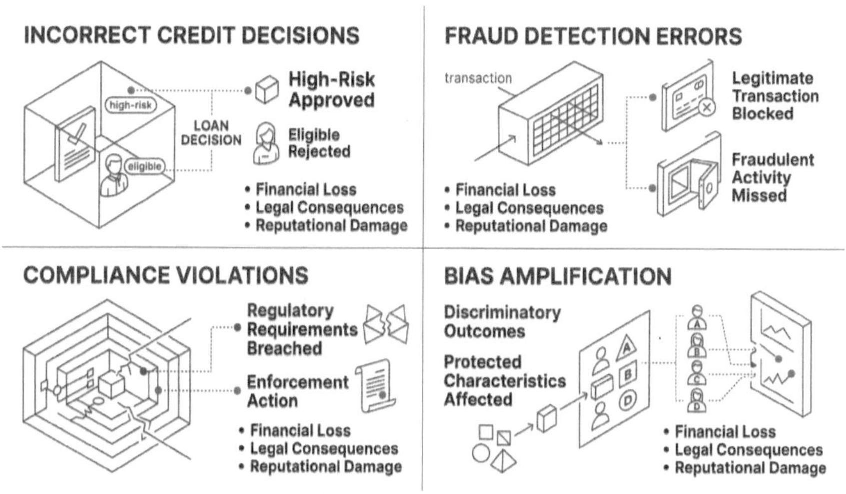

⊗ Every failure scenario in BFSI triggers consequences across three dimensions simultaneously financial, legal, and reputational. There is no low-stakes AI failure in this sector.

Risk Management & Third-Party AI

AI systems must integrate with enterprise risk frameworks and compliance processes as a first-class requirement not an afterthought. Risk must be systematically identified, assessed, and mitigated. Third-party AI introduces an additional layer of challenge.

Enterprise Risk Integration

Every AI system must map directly to the organisation's risk taxonomy. This means embedding AI outputs into existing risk dashboards, escalation pathways, and governance committees not operating as a parallel, disconnected function.

Third-Party AI Risks

- Data exposure through external model access
- Lack of transparency into model logic and training
- Compliance challenges across jurisdictional boundaries

Validate Outputs

Test third-party models against internal standards before deployment.

Monitor Behaviour

Continuously track third-party AI outputs for drift and anomalies.

Contractual Safeguards

Ensure vendor agreements include audit rights and compliance obligations.

From Automation to Controlled Decision Systems

The strategic imperative for BFSI is clear: move from automated decision-making to **controlled, auditable, and explainable decision systems**. AI will increase decision speed, expand into new areas, and drive genuine innovation but success in BFSI depends entirely on control, compliance, and trust.

1

Balance Automation with Control

Speed and scale must never outpace the governance structures that protect customers and institutions.

2

Align AI with Regulatory Frameworks

Compliance is not a constraint to work around it is the design specification for BFSI AI.

3

Build Trust Through Transparency

Organisations that earn trust through explainability and accountability will define the future of AI in finance.

In BFSI, AI decisions are not just technical outcomes. They are financial commitments, regulatory events, and trust signals. The future of AI in finance will not be defined by how fast it decides but by how responsibly it does so

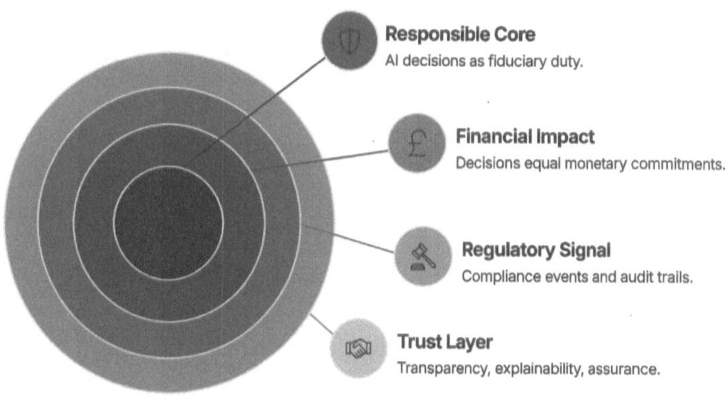

Chapter 27

The Future: AI That Asks Permission

For most of its evolution, AI has followed a simple model: learn, optimise, execute. It does not ask, pause, or seek approval it acts. As AI systems grow more powerful, the next phase of evolution is becoming clear. AI must not only decide it must know **when not to decide.** This chapter explores the shift from autonomous execution to controlled intelligence, and the design philosophy that makes it possible.

The Current Paradigm vs. The Future

The dominant model of AI behaviour has always privileged action. If a system can act, it should act. Speed, scale, and efficiency have been the primary measures of success but they have come at a cost.

Today's Paradigm

"If the system can act, it should act."

- Learn from data
- Optimise outcomes
- Execute decisions

Enables speed, scale, and efficiency but introduces risk, misalignment, and loss of control.

The Future Paradigm

"The system should act only when it is allowed to act."

- Evaluate authority to act
- Check boundaries and thresholds
- Escalate when required

Introduces **permission-aware AI** a system that exercises structured restraint before execution.

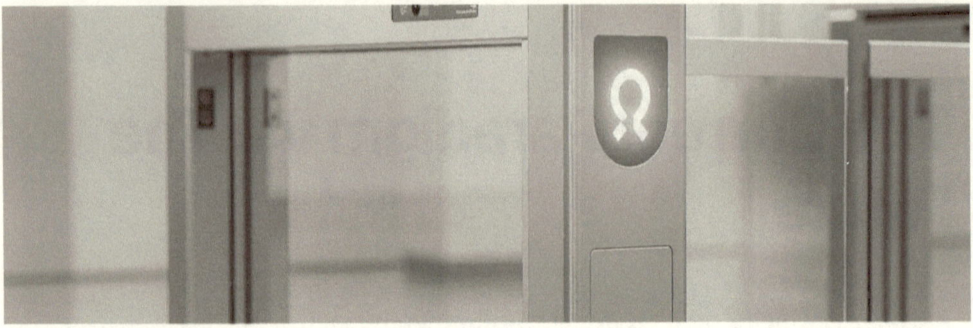

What "Asking Permission" Really Means

Permission-aware AI does not mean a system that literally poses questions. It means AI systems that evaluate whether they are **authorised to act** under current conditions before any execution occurs.

Before executing a decision, a permission-aware system assesses four critical questions:

1

Boundary Check

Is this action within my defined operational boundaries?

2

Confidence Threshold

Does this decision meet the required certainty level?

3

Escalation Trigger

Does this require human review before proceeding?

4

Policy Compliance

Are there governance constraints that restrict this action?

The Decision Gate Concept

Future AI systems will incorporate **decision gates** structured checkpoints that sit between a potential action and its execution. Rather than acting immediately, the system evaluates context, checks boundaries, and determines the appropriate path forward.

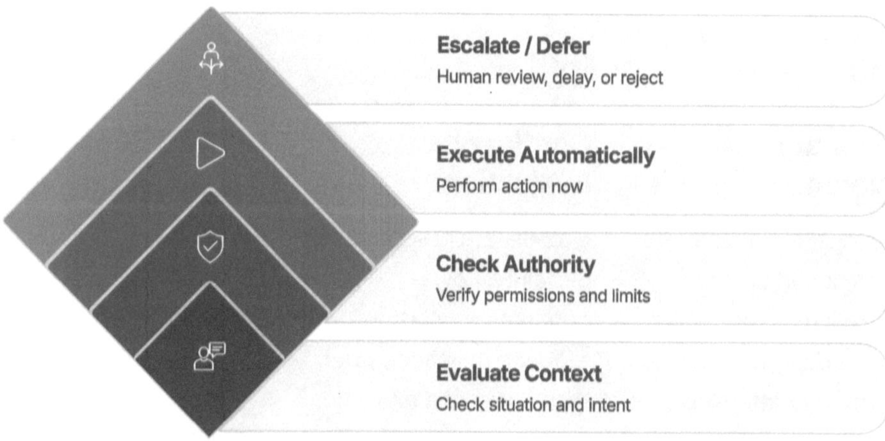

Decision gates transform AI from a pure executor into a controlled agent one that produces outcomes only when conditions for authorised action are genuinely met. This single architectural addition changes the fundamental nature of how AI systems interact with risk.

Key Capabilities of Permission-Aware AI

Implementing permission-aware behaviour requires five distinct capabilities embedded into the system's architecture. These are not model-level features they are design-level properties.

Boundary Awareness

The system understands where it can act and where it must not. Operational limits are explicit, not inferred.

Confidence Evaluation

Outputs are assessed for certainty. Low-confidence decisions trigger escalation rather than automatic execution.

Context Sensitivity

The system considers environment and scenario complexity before determining whether action is appropriate.

Escalation Intelligence

The system identifies when human involvement is required and routes decisions accordingly without prompting.

Self-Constraint

The system actively limits its own actions not because it cannot act, but because it recognises it should not.

From Optimisation to Judgment

Today's AI optimises. It finds the best path to a defined objective with remarkable speed and consistency. But optimisation without judgment is brittle it fails when context shifts, ambiguity arises, or the objective itself is incomplete.

Future AI must incorporate **judgment-like behaviour** not human judgment, but structured decision evaluation that mirrors its essential qualities. This means:

→ **Assessing Uncertainty**

Recognising when outputs are unreliable and flagging them accordingly.

→ **Recognising Limits**

Understanding the boundary of the system's own competence.

→ **Handling Ambiguity**

Deferring or escalating when situations fall outside defined parameters.

Control Architecture: The Foundation

Permission-aware AI is not achieved through better models. It requires better **system design**. The architecture surrounding the model must encode the constraints, escalation paths, and control points that make restrained behaviour possible.

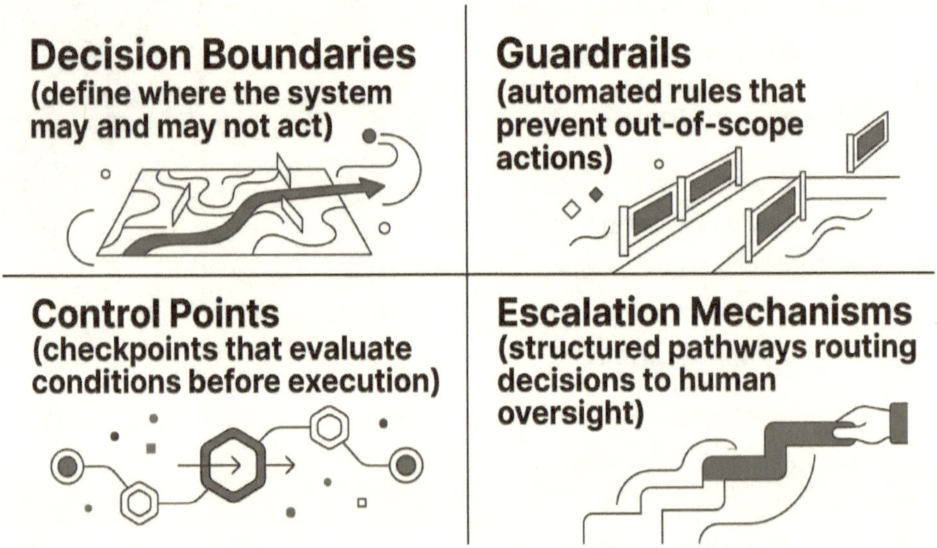

> ⓘ Control architecture is not a layer added on top of AI it is the structure within which AI operates. Organisations that treat it as an afterthought will find permission-awareness impossible to implement at scale.

Benefits, Challenges & The Strategic Imperative

Permission-aware AI delivers measurable organisational benefits but implementation is not without complexity. Understanding both sides is essential for realistic adoption planning.

✓ Reduced Risk

Prevents incorrect or unauthorised actions before they occur.

✓ Improved Trust

Transparent decision-making builds confidence with stakeholders.

✓ Better Alignment

Decisions consistently reflect organisational intent and policy.

✓ Scalable Control

Maintains governance efficiency as systems grow in scope.

⚠ Complexity

Designing effective decision gates requires significant architectural investment.

⚠ Latency

Evaluating conditions in real time introduces processing overhead.

⚠ Defining Boundaries

Translating organisational intent into machine-readable rules is non-trivial.

⚠ Integration

Embedding control architecture into existing systems demands coordination across teams.

⚠ Organisations must prepare now regulatory expectations, customer trust demands, and system complexity are converging. Those who delay will face adoption friction at a scale that is difficult to recover from.

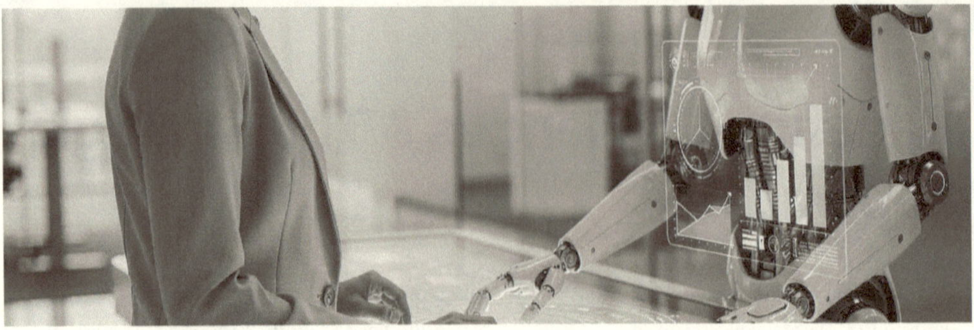

Human–AI Collaboration: A New Dynamic

Permission-aware AI fundamentally reshapes the relationship between human decision-makers and automated systems. The model shifts from passive monitoring to active collaboration humans engage when their judgment is genuinely needed, not as a fallback for system failure.

1. **Today**

   AI executes. Humans monitor for errors after the fact.

2. **Transition**

   AI flags uncertainty. Humans review escalated decisions selectively.

3. **Future**

   AI evaluates permission. Humans decide only when the system determines it is required.

The result is a **collaborative decision system** one where automation handles volume and speed, while human judgment is reserved for situations that genuinely demand it. This is not a reduction in human authority; it is a more precise deployment of it.

The Closing Thought: Restraint as the Highest Capability

> The ultimate evolution of AI is not intelligence. It is restraint. The most advanced system is not the one that acts the fastest but the one that knows when to pause.

The shift from capability to responsibility is not a constraint on AI's potential. It is the condition that makes AI's potential trustworthy enough to deploy at scale. Permission-aware systems built on control architecture, decision gates, and structured judgment are the foundation for autonomous systems that organisations, regulators, and the public can genuinely rely on.

Safe	Scalable	Aligned
Prevents harm through authorised action boundaries.	Maintains governance efficiency as deployment grows.	Decisions consistently reflect human intent and organisational values.

- Capability → Control → Intelligence → Responsibility. This is the arc of AI evolution. Organisations that design for restraint today will lead the responsible AI systems of tomorrow.

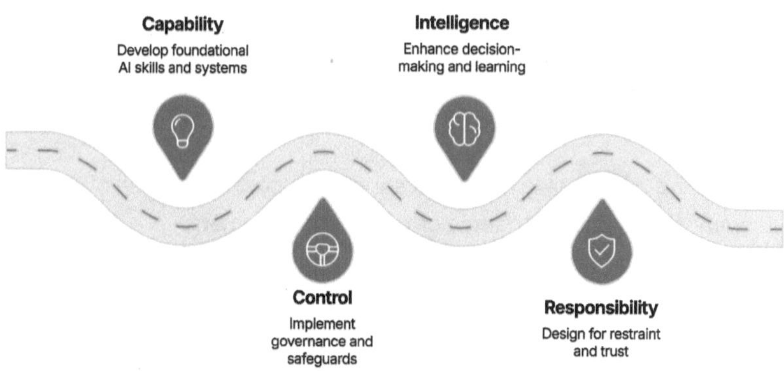

Chapter 28

Economics of Control

For most organisations, control is framed as a constraint something that slows systems down, introduces friction, and increases cost. The instinct, therefore, is to optimise first and govern later. This chapter challenges that assumption directly. In AI systems, lack of control does not eliminate cost. It delays and amplifies it. Control is not a cost centre. It is an economic lever and understanding it as such is the foundation of sustainable AI at scale.

The Misconception: Cost vs. Control

Organisations frequently perceive a direct trade-off between control and efficiency. This perception is not only incorrect it is economically dangerous. The error lies in evaluating control exclusively in the short term, whilst ignoring the delayed and cumulative costs that uncontrolled systems generate.

Perception	Reality
• More control → higher cost • Less control → higher efficiency • Control slows growth	• More control → lower long-term cost • Less control → hidden inefficiency • Lack of control creates risk drag

⚠ Evaluating control only through a short-term cost lens is one of the most common and costly strategic errors in AI deployment.

Understanding the Economics of AI Systems

AI systems generate value through automation, optimisation, and scale. But they simultaneously generate risk, error, and variability. The economic outcome of any AI deployment is determined by the balance between value creation and risk exposure a balance that control mechanisms directly govern.

Value Generation

- Automation of repetitive tasks
- Optimisation of decisions at speed
- Scale beyond human capacity

Risk Exposure

- Compounding error rates
- Systemic variability and drift
- Downstream cascading failures

The economic outcome depends entirely on the balance between these two forces. Control is the mechanism that maintains it.

The Cost Components of Uncontrolled AI

The costs of uncontrolled AI systems are often hidden, delayed, and cumulative making them easy to underestimate until they become critical. Across five distinct dimensions, the financial exposure compounds over time.

1. **Direct Financial Loss**

   Incorrect decisions, revenue leakage, and fraud misclassification create immediate but often untracked monetary impact.

2. **Operational Inefficiency**

   Manual corrections, system rework, and elevated support costs consume resources that scale with system adoption.

3. **Reputational Damage**

   Customer trust erosion and brand impact are difficult to quantify but deeply consequential over the long term.

4. **Regulatory Penalties**

   Fines and compliance costs are increasingly significant as AI governance frameworks mature globally.

5. **Opportunity Cost**

   Missed revenue and suboptimal decisions represent the silent cost of systems that underperform due to unchecked variability.

The Cost Curve: Two Trajectories

The economic difference between controlled and uncontrolled AI is most clearly illustrated through diverging cost trajectories over time. Without governance, costs begin low but escalate exponentially as errors compound, incidents accumulate, and remediation becomes reactive. With control in place, a moderate upfront investment yields a stable and declining total cost profile.

Uncontrolled Path

Low initial cost. High long-term cost. Reactive remediation that escalates with scale and complexity.

Controlled Path

Moderate upfront investment. Lower total cost over time. Prevention replaces remediation as the primary cost driver.

> Control shifts cost from reactive to preventive the single most important economic insight in AI governance.

Return on Control (ROC)

Organisations deploying AI at scale need a framework for evaluating the value of governance investment. Return on Control (ROC) provides that lens moving the conversation from "what does control cost?" to "what does control deliver?"

Reduction in Risk Cost

Fewer incidents, lower remediation expenditure, and reduced regulatory exposure directly lower the total cost of AI operation.

Improved Decision Quality

Control mechanisms reduce variability, improving the consistency and accuracy of AI-driven outcomes across the organisation.

Increased System Reliability

Stable, predictable systems reduce operational overhead and build the internal confidence needed to scale AI adoption further.

Key Economic Drivers of Control

Three forces determine how urgently and extensively control must be applied. Each amplifies both the value AI creates and the risk it exposes making control not optional, but structurally necessary as systems mature.

Scale

Higher scale amplifies both value and risk. Control ensures risk does not outpace value creation.

Speed

Faster decisions increase efficiency but also increase risk exposure. Control balances speed with safety.

Complexity

More complex systems carry higher uncertainty. Control reduces unpredictability across interconnected components.

As scale, speed, and complexity increase together as they inevitably do in maturing AI programmes the economic case for control strengthens proportionally.

Finding the Balance: Investment & Optimal Control

Control requires investment across four domains: architecture (control points and guardrails), observability (logging and monitoring), governance (policies and processes), and talent (skilled teams). But investment must be calibrated. Both underinvestment and over-control carry distinct economic penalties.

Cost of Underinvestment

- Increased incidents and failures
- Higher remediation cost
- Erosion of stakeholder trust

Cost of Over-Control

- Reduced system performance
- Increased latency
- Innovation constrained unnecessarily

The Goal: Optimal Control

The objective is not maximum control it is optimal control. The right balance is determined by risk appetite, industry requirements, and system impact.

Organisations that calibrate correctly deploy faster, scale safely, and earn regulatory trust converting control into a genuine competitive advantage.

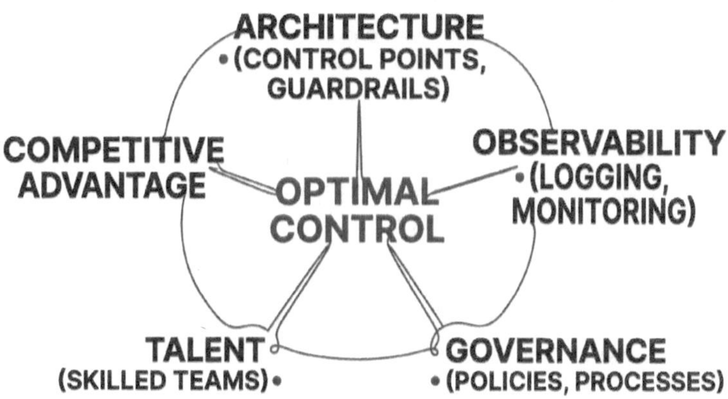

Key Takeaways

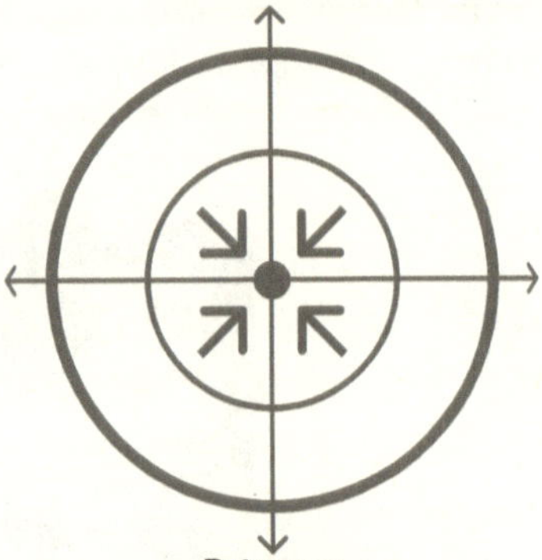

Control is an economic lever not a cost burden

Framing control as overhead misrepresents its function. It is a value-generating mechanism when applied correctly.

Uncontrolled AI creates hidden and cumulative cost

The absence of governance does not reduce cost it defers and amplifies it across financial, operational, and reputational dimensions.

Control enables competitive advantage

Organisations with strong governance deploy with greater confidence, scale more safely, and build the regulatory trust that accelerates adoption.

> AI systems create value at scale. But scale without control creates risk at scale. The organisations that win will not be those that build the fastest systems but those that build the most controlled ones.

Chapter 29

Leadership in the Autonomous Era

Technology transformations are often framed as engineering challenges. This one is not. AI is not just changing systems it is changing how decisions are made. And when decisions change, leadership must evolve. The leaders who succeed will not be those who make the most decisions, but those who design the best decision systems.

The Fundamental Shift

For decades, leaders have set direction, allocated resources, and reviewed outcomes. In an AI-driven world, the ground has shifted beneath that model entirely.

Traditional Leadership

- Strategy and direction-setting
- Execution oversight
- Performance review
- Human decision-making at every step

Leadership in the Autonomous Era

- Decisions executed by systems
- Actions at machine speed
- Outcomes emerging continuously
- Control over decision architecture

Leadership is no longer about making every decision. It is about designing how decisions are made.

From Decision-Makers to System Designers

The most profound shift for executive leaders is not adopting new tools it is adopting a new identity. Leaders must move from direct decision-making to designing the frameworks within which decisions are made.

1. **Direct Decisions**

   Leader decides each outcome individually

2. **Decision Frameworks**

   Leader designs policies, constraints, and thresholds

3. **System Alignment**

   AI operates within intent-driven boundaries at scale

This includes defining policies, setting risk thresholds, and establishing control mechanisms that govern autonomous system behaviour across the entire organisation.

New Leadership Responsibilities

Autonomous systems demand that leaders take ownership of five core responsibilities that did not exist in traditional operating models.

1

Define Intent Clearly

AI systems require explicit objectives and clear constraints. Intent must be unambiguous and measurable ambiguity at the top becomes unpredictability at scale.

2

Set Boundaries

Define precisely what AI can decide autonomously and what requires human oversight. Boundaries are not limitations they are the architecture of trust.

3

Align Systems with Strategy

Ensure that AI decisions consistently reflect business goals. Misaligned systems silently erode strategic direction.

4

Balance Speed and Control

Leaders must make deliberate choices about where speed is the competitive advantage and where control is the non-negotiable requirement.

5

Manage Risk Continuously

AI introduces continuous, emergent risk. Leaders must define risk appetite and ensure mitigation is embedded not bolted on.

The Leadership Control Framework

Effective leaders operating in the autonomous era focus their attention across four interconnected areas. This framework mirrors the Four-Layer Governance Model and translates governance principles into leadership action.

1. Policy

Define intent and establish organisational direction for AI systems.

2. Process

Structure workflows that govern how AI decisions are made and reviewed.

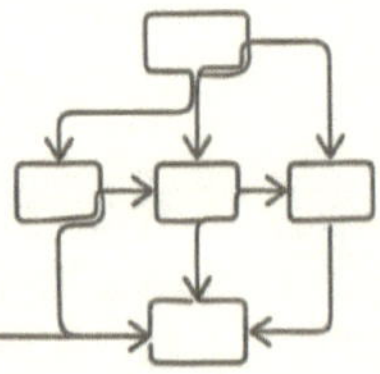

3. Enforcement

Ensure execution of policies through monitoring and accountability mechanisms.

4. Interface

Enable meaningful human oversight and intervention points.

> ⓘ This framework does not replace governance structures it ensures leaders are actively engaged in making those structures effective and strategically aligned.

Decision Ownership & Organisational Culture

Who Owns the Decision?

Even when AI acts, accountability remains human. Leadership must redefine who owns decisions and who is accountable for outcomes regardless of whether a system or a person executed the action.

- Clarify human accountability at every layer
- Document decision authority explicitly
- Ensure escalation paths are unambiguous

The Cultural Shift Required

Organisations must move from a speed-first mindset to a control-aware mindset. This is a cultural transformation, not a policy exercise.

- Embed responsible AI practices organisation-wide
- Build awareness of risk at every level
- Align day-to-day behaviour with governance principles

> Without leadership alignment, systems evolve without control, decisions drift from intent, and risk accumulates silently until it becomes a crisis.

Key Leadership Capabilities for the Autonomous Era

Succeeding as a leader in an AI-driven organisation requires cultivating four distinct capabilities none of which require deep technical expertise, but all of which require deliberate development.

Systems Thinking

Understanding end-to-end system behaviour and how individual decisions cascade across the organisation.

Technical Awareness

Not coding but understanding the implications of system design choices and their strategic consequences.

Risk Intelligence

Identifying, assessing, and managing the continuous and emergent risks that AI systems introduce.

Decision Design

Structuring how decisions are made defining policies, constraints, thresholds, and human touchpoints.

The Strategic Advantage of Leadership Control

Governance defines the rules. Leadership ensures those rules are effective and aligned with strategy. Organisations that close the gap between the two gain a decisive competitive advantage in the autonomous era.

Deploy Responsibly

Strong leadership enables confident, ethical AI deployment at every level of the organisation.

Scale with Confidence

Control frameworks allow organisations to expand AI use cases without accumulating hidden risk.

Maintain Trust

Stakeholders, regulators, and customers trust organisations where humans remain accountable.

> In the autonomous era, leadership is not defined by control over people. It is defined by control over systems that make decisions.

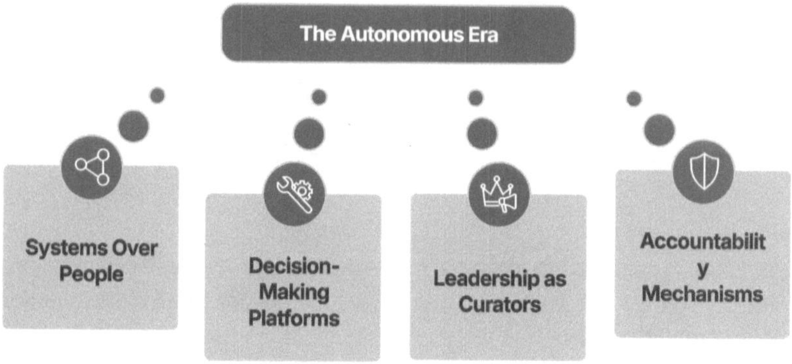

Chapter 30

CTO Roadmap to 2035

AI is no longer just recommending it is deciding, acting, and scaling decisions continuously. This final synthesis maps the strategic journey every technology leader must take from deploying AI capability to mastering AI control at scale. The organisations that win the next decade will not simply build intelligent systems. They will build systems that know how to control themselves.

The Strategic Shift: From Intelligence to Execution

Across industries, one pattern has become undeniable. AI systems are no longer passive advisors they are active participants in operational decision-making. This is a fundamental change in the nature of enterprise technology.

Recommending	Deciding
AI surfaces insights and options for human review. Humans remain fully in the loop for every decision.	AI selects outcomes autonomously within defined boundaries. Human oversight becomes selective and strategic.
Acting	**Scaling**
AI executes decisions end-to-end, triggering downstream processes without manual approval.	AI replicates decisions continuously across millions of interactions, far beyond any human capacity.

> By 2035, AI systems will make the majority of operational decisions. Human intervention will be selective and strategic. **Control becomes the foundation of digital infrastructure.**

Every Organisation Becomes a Decision System

The shift is not confined to technology companies. Across every sector, organisations are transitioning from connectivity and data collection into fully operational decision systems. The question is no longer whether this transformation will happen but whether it will be controlled.

Telecom

Networks evolve from passive carriers into decision-driven infrastructure routing, prioritising, and optimising autonomously in real time.

BFSI

Financial systems become regulated decision engines automating credit, risk, fraud detection, and compliance at unprecedented scale.

Enterprise

Operational platforms automate supply chains, workforce decisions, and customer interactions across complex global organisations.

The CTO Mandate: Three Core Responsibilities

The role of the CTO must evolve in response to this new reality. Deploying models is no longer sufficient. The mandate now encompasses three interconnected responsibilities that must be held in constant balance.

1

Build AI Capability

- Deploy models at production scale
- Enable end-to-end automation
- Scale intelligence across the enterprise

2

Ensure Control

- Define clear boundaries of autonomy
- Embed guardrails into system design
- Implement layered control architecture

3

Maintain Alignment

- Align AI decisions with business strategy
- Manage risk across the decision portfolio
- Ensure ongoing regulatory compliance

> The CTO's challenge is no longer *how to deploy AI* it is *how to control AI at scale.*

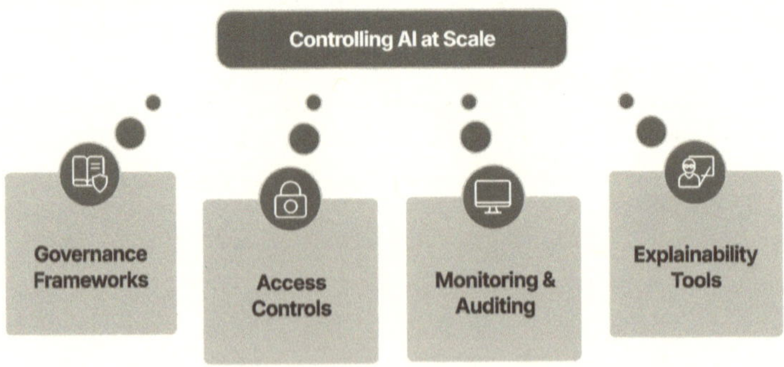

The Control Architecture

A controlled AI system is not built from a single mechanism. It requires a layered architecture where each level reinforces the others from defining intent at the top to enabling human oversight at the interface.

The Control Stack

Four integrated layers form the foundation of AI governance in any production system.

- **Policy Layer** Define organisational intent
- **Process Layer** Translate intent into workflows
- **Enforcement Layer** Apply control at runtime
- **Interface Layer** Enable human oversight

The Six Control Mechanisms

→ **Decision Boundaries**

Define the precise limits of AI autonomy

→ **Control Points & Guardrails**

Embed intervention locations; enforce constraints in real time

→ **Kill Switches & Escalation**

Enable human intervention at any point in the decision chain

→ **Observability & Auditability**

Ensure full visibility and accountability across all decisions

The Transformation Roadmap: 2025 → 2035

The journey to controlled AI autonomy unfolds across four distinct phases. Each phase builds on the last deepening capability, embedding control, and ultimately enabling systems that govern themselves.

1

Phase 1 · 2025–2027

Awareness & Foundation

Establish policies, identify AI systems, begin monitoring. Target: Level 1–2 maturity.

2

Phase 2 · 2027–2030

Control Integration

Implement control points, deploy guardrails, establish escalation paths. Target: Level 3 maturity.

3

Phase 3 · 2030–2033

Adaptive Systems

Real-time monitoring, drift detection, dynamic boundaries. Target: Level 4 maturity.

4

Phase 4 · 2033–2035

Autonomous Control

AI-driven control mechanisms, automated escalation decisions. Target: Level 5 maturity.

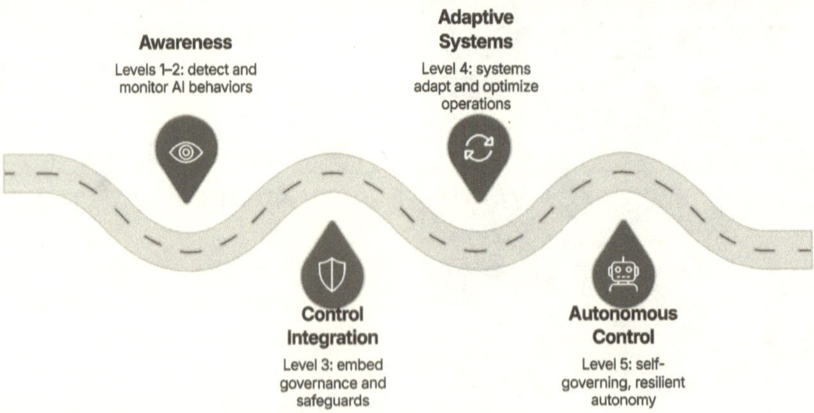

Investment Priorities: Technology & Organisation

Achieving AI control by 2035 requires deliberate investment across two dimensions the technical infrastructure that enables control, and the organisational capabilities that sustain it. Neither is sufficient alone.

Technology Priorities

AI Infrastructure

Scalable, production-grade platforms for model deployment and management

Control Architecture

Guardrails, enforcement layers, and policy engines embedded at every level

Observability Systems

Logging, tracing, and explainability tooling for full decision transparency

Integration Platforms

MLOps and DevOps pipelines that bake control into continuous delivery

Organisational Priorities

Governance Model

Clear ownership structures and defined roles for AI accountability across the enterprise

Talent Strategy

AI engineers, risk specialists, and governance practitioners embedded in product teams

Risk Management

Defined risk appetite, continuous monitoring, and integrated risk frameworks

Control Culture

A control-aware mindset embedded across engineering, product, and leadership

The Strategic Case for Control

Control is not a cost centre it is a competitive differentiator. Organisations that invest early in AI governance and control architecture will outperform those that treat it as a compliance afterthought.

5

Maturity Levels

From awareness to full autonomous control each level unlocks greater capability with confidence

2035

Target Horizon

The year leading organisations achieve self-regulating, fully governed AI decision systems

4

Investment Areas

Infrastructure, control architecture, observability, and integration the core technology stack

The Cost Equation

Control shifts the financial model from **reactive cost** to **preventive investment**. Organisations that invest early reduce long-term remediation costs and increase system reliability delivering compounding returns over time.

Competitive Advantage

Organisations with strong AI control frameworks are able to:

- **Deploy faster** with confidence in system behaviour
- **Scale safely** without exponential risk accumulation
- **Gain regulatory trust** as a durable market advantage

> The future will belong to those who do not just build intelligent systems but build systems that know how to control themselves.

ANNEXURE A

AI Control Quick Checklist

A practical framework for organizations to rapidly assess whether their AI systems are **governed, observable, controlled, and accountable**. Designed for CTOs, AI leaders, enterprise architects, governance teams, and risk & compliance functions.

Governed

Formal frameworks, policies, and executive ownership in place

Observable

Logging, monitoring, and audit trails actively maintained

Controlled

Runtime guardrails, kill switches, and decision boundaries defined

Accountable

Clear human ownership, escalation paths, and compliance mapping

> AI governance is not validated by documentation. It is validated by operational control.

Governance, Ownership & Data

Strategy & Governance

- AI governance framework formally defined
- Executive ownership assigned for AI systems
- AI risk appetite documented
- Policies mapped to operational systems
- AI usage inventory maintained

Decision Ownership

- Clear ownership defined for AI decisions
- Human accountability documented
- Escalation responsibilities assigned
- High-impact decisions identified

Data Governance

- Data sources validated & lineage traceable
- Sensitive data handling defined
- Data quality monitoring enabled
- Access controls implemented

Model Governance

- Model validation & bias testing performed
- Explainability requirements defined
- Drift monitoring & version control active

Runtime Control

- Decision boundaries & guardrails configured
- Confidence thresholds defined
- Kill switch & real-time intervention available

Observability

- Decision logging & audit trails maintained
- Alerts and anomaly detection configured
- Incident monitoring active

Oversight, Third-Party & Compliance

Human Oversight

- Human-in-the-loop processes defined
- Escalation triggers documented
- Override capability available
- Manual intervention workflows tested

Third-Party AI Governance

- External AI vendors assessed
- Output validation implemented
- Vendor risk management established
- Third-party monitoring active
- Contractual accountability defined

Compliance & Risk

- Regulatory requirements mapped
- AI risk assessments conducted
- Compliance monitoring active
- Incident response plan documented
- Business continuity plans tested

Organizational Readiness

- AI governance training conducted
- Cross-functional coordination established
- AI ethics awareness promoted
- AI control KPIs defined
- Continuous improvement process active

Quick Scoring Model & Maturity Levels

Each completed checkpoint contributes to an overall score. Use the scale below to determine your organization's AI control maturity and identify priority gaps.

Score	Maturity Level
0–20	Initial / Ad Hoc
21–40	Emerging
41–60	Managed
61–80	Controlled
81–100	Optimized

Below 40

Significant control gaps immediate action required

40–70

Partial governance maturity targeted improvements needed

Above 70

Strong operational AI control foundations established

Key Insight: AI governance is not validated by documentation. It is validated by **operational control** the ability to observe, intervene, and enforce accountability in real time.

Annexure B

Decision Escalation Model

As AI systems become increasingly autonomous, organizations require structured mechanisms to govern when AI may act independently, when decisions require human review, and when systems must halt or escalate. This framework establishes a controlled, tiered approach to autonomous decision-making balancing operational efficiency with accountability, auditability, and risk management.

The Escalation Pyramid

The model organizes AI decisions into five discrete levels, from fully autonomous informational outputs to critical actions requiring executive multi-party authorization. Each level defines AI authority, human involvement, and control requirements.

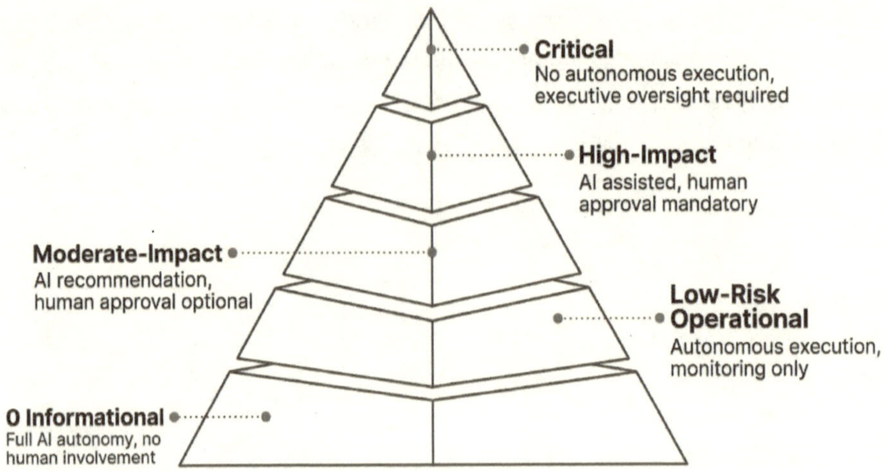

Autonomy decreases and human oversight increases as decisions move up the pyramid. The model ensures that consequential, irreversible, or strategically sensitive actions are never executed without appropriate authorization.

Decision Levels in Detail

Each level carries distinct characteristics, representative use cases, and governance requirements. Understanding these distinctions is essential for correct implementation across enterprise AI systems.

Level	Decision Type	Examples	AI Authority	Human Involvement
0	Informational	Reporting, notifications, analytics summaries	Full autonomy	None
1	Low-Risk Operational	Traffic optimization, routine automation, recommendation ranking	Autonomous execution	Monitoring & logging
2	Moderate-Impact	Customer prioritization, resource allocation, dynamic pricing	AI recommendation	Human approval optional
3	High-Impact	Credit approvals, security actions, service restrictions	AI assisted	Approval mandatory
4	Critical	Infrastructure shutdown, healthcare interventions, executive financial actions	No autonomous execution	Executive oversight

Core Escalation Triggers

AI systems must initiate escalation automatically when predefined conditions are detected. These triggers serve as the operational backbone of the escalation model, ensuring that boundary violations surface for human review before irreversible action is taken.

Confidence Drops Below Threshold

When prediction confidence falls below a defined threshold, the system cannot act with sufficient certainty and must defer to human judgment.

Policy Conflict Detected

A proposed decision violates an active governance rule, regulatory constraint, or organizational policy requiring review before execution.

Unusual Patterns Detected

Behavioral anomalies in input data or model outputs signal that conditions fall outside the system's validated operational envelope.

Risk Threshold Exceeded

Financial exposure, liability, or operational consequence surpasses the pre-approved ceiling for autonomous action at the current decision level.

System Uncertainty Increases

Insufficient contextual data or conflicting signals prevent the system from making a reliable determination, necessitating human-in-the-loop review.

Escalation Workflow

When a decision is initiated, the AI system follows a structured six-step workflow to evaluate, validate, and route the action appropriately. Human review is triggered only when required preserving operational efficiency while enforcing governance guardrails.

The Role of Human Oversight

Human oversight remains non-negotiable for ambiguous decisions, ethical trade-offs, regulatory-sensitive actions, and situations where strategic judgment supersedes algorithmic confidence.

When Oversight Is Triggered

- Ambiguous or ethically complex decisions
- Actions with regulatory implications
- Strategic trade-offs requiring executive judgment
- Any Level 3 or Level 4 classification

Guiding Principle & Implementation Considerations

> **Autonomy should increase only when confidence, observability, and control maturity increase.** Core Principle, Decision Escalation Model

This principle anchors the entire framework. Expanding AI autonomy is not a default outcome of deployment maturity it must be earned through demonstrated reliability, robust monitoring infrastructure, and validated control mechanisms at each level.

Confidence

Model outputs must meet statistically validated thresholds before operating at higher autonomy levels.

Observability

Full logging, real-time monitoring, and audit trail requirements must be satisfied across all active decision levels.

Control Maturity

Governance controls including escalation paths, override mechanisms, and policy enforcement must be operationally proven before autonomy is extended.

ⓘ Organizations implementing this model should conduct periodic level-calibration reviews to ensure decision classifications remain aligned with current risk appetite, regulatory requirements, and AI system capability assessments.

Annexure C

Glossary of AI Control & Governance

A definitive reference of core terminology used across AI control frameworks, governance structures, and enterprise deployment contexts. These definitions establish the shared language for risk, compliance, and AI governance professionals operating in enterprise environments.

Foundational Concepts

AI Control

The mechanisms, frameworks, and operational systems used to govern how AI systems make and execute decisions.

Autonomous System

A system capable of making and executing decisions with limited or no human intervention.

Controlled Autonomy

A model where AI systems operate autonomously within predefined boundaries and control mechanisms.

Decision Infrastructure

Systems where AI becomes embedded into operational decision-making processes at scale.

Governance Layer Terms

- **AI** governance policies, frameworks, processes, and controls used to manage AI responsibly.
- **Policy Layer** Defines objectives, constraints, and acceptable AI behavior.
- **Enforcement Layer** Implements real-time AI controls and restrictions operationally.
- **Risk Appetite** The level of risk an organization is willing to accept when deploying AI systems.

Operational Control Terms

- **Decision Boundary** A predefined limit defining where AI may act autonomously versus where escalation is required.
- **Runtime Guardrail** A real-time enforcement mechanism constraining AI system behavior during operation.
- **Kill Switch** A mechanism allowing immediate interruption or shutdown of autonomous AI operations.
- **Escalation Mechanism** Routes decisions to higher authority or human oversight under defined conditions.

Observability, Maturity & Extended Terms

Observability

The ability to monitor, trace, and understand AI system behavior in real time.

Auditability

The capability to reconstruct and verify how an AI decision was made.

Explainability

The ability to understand and communicate how an AI system arrived at a decision.

Human-in-the-Loop (HITL)

A governance approach where humans participate in reviewing, approving, or overriding AI decisions.

Term	Definition
AI Drift	A condition where AI model performance or behavior changes over time due to evolving data or conditions.
Permission-Aware AI	AI systems capable of evaluating whether they are authorized to act under current conditions.
AI Control Maturity Model	A framework used to evaluate organizational maturity in governing and controlling AI systems.
Third-Party AI	AI models, APIs, or intelligent systems provided by external vendors or service providers.
Enterprise AI	The deployment of AI systems across organizational processes, operations, infrastructure, and decision-making environments.

> This glossary is an annexure to the primary AI governance framework. All terms defined herein are authoritative references for policy drafting, audit procedures, and enterprise AI risk assessments.

Annexure D

References

This reference section provides the foundational books, standards, frameworks, and research themes that shaped the ideas throughout this book. The scope is intentionally **interdisciplinary** because AI control itself is an interdisciplinary challenge.

Artificial Intelligence

Alignment, autonomy & decision systems

Governance & Ethics

Enterprise control & accountability

Telecom & Infrastructure

Autonomous networks & transformation

Risk & Systems

Decision theory & architecture

📕 Books & Foundational Reading

Seven essential texts spanning AI risk, alignment, decision-making, and systemic uncertainty.

Superintelligence Nick Bostrom

Foundational exploration of advanced AI risks and long-term control problems.

Human Compatible Stuart Russell

Building AI aligned with human values and uncertainty-aware objectives.

The Alignment Problem Brian Christian

How ML systems diverge from intended human objectives.

Life 3.0 Max Tegmark

Societal, economic, and existential implications of advanced AI.

Thinking, Fast and Slow

Kahneman Human bias & decision-making

Gödel, Escher, Bach

Hofstadter Intelligence, recursion & consciousness

The Black Swan

Taleb Non-linear risk & systemic fragility

🌐 AI Governance & Ethics Frameworks

Five major global frameworks shaping trustworthy, accountable, and human-centered AI governance.

1	**OECD AI Principles** Transparency, accountability, and human-centered values for trustworthy AI.
2	**NIST AI RMF** Operational risk governance: **Govern · Map · Measure · Manage**
3	**EU AI Act** Risk classification, high-risk AI systems, accountability and transparency.
4	**UNESCO AI Ethics** Global guidance on human rights, inclusion, and governance.
5	**IEEE Ethically Aligned Design** Responsible autonomous and intelligent systems framework.

Enterprise Governance

- COBIT Framework operational governance structures
- ITIL & Service Governance AI operations management
- ISO/IEC 42001 AI Management System Standard
- ISO 31000 Enterprise risk management integration

Cloud & AI Infrastructure

- **MLOps** model lifecycle, deployment governance, continuous monitoring
- **DevSecOps** security-integrated operational engineering for runtime control

📡 Telecom, AI Systems & Cybersecurity

3GPP Standards

AI-native networks, NWDAF, and autonomous telecom systems. Groups: SA1, SA2, SA5, RAN.

ETSI ZSM

Zero-Touch Network & Service Management closed-loop automation for autonomous telecom ops.

TM Forum

Autonomous Networks maturity models and operational frameworks for telecom systems.

Reinforcement Learning

Optimization behavior, reward functions, and autonomous learning systems.

HITL Research

Human-in-the-Loop: controlled autonomy, escalation frameworks, hybrid decision systems.

Zero Trust & Defense-in-Depth

Runtime enforcement, continuous validation, and layered AI control architectures.

🧠 Philosophical, Economic & Conceptual Influences

Cybernetics Norbert Wiener

Foundational control systems, feedback loops, and machine behavior.

Systems Theory Ludwig von Bertalanffy

Interconnected and adaptive systems thinking.

Decision Theory

Escalation models, risk evaluation, and autonomous decision systems.

Platform Economy & Digital Infrastructure

AI as infrastructure, decision platforms, and enterprise operating models.

Systems Thinking & Complexity Theory

Adaptive systems, emergent behavior, and non-linear interactions.

✍️ Author's Prior Works

Key themes in this book build on the author's earlier titles:

- Moral Code: Ethics at the Heart of AI
- Threshold Breach: When Artificial Intelligence Decides
- 6G Threshold: From Connectivity to Decision-Driven Networks
- Entangled Realities

Collectively examining AI ethics, autonomous systems, infrastructure intelligence, and governance.

Final Reflection

> The future of AI will depend not only on how intelligently systems operate but on how responsibly humanity designs the systems that govern them.

This book draws from multiple disciplines because AI control cannot be solved through technology alone. It demands integration across engineering, governance, leadership, ethics, risk management, and systems architecture.

⚠ AI governance standards are evolving rapidly. Readers are encouraged to continuously monitor emerging regulations, track new frameworks, and adapt operational models as the field matures.

Engineering	Governance	Ethics
Risk Management	Systems Architecture	

The Final Reflection

Epilogue AI CONTROL: From Intelligence to Accountable Systems

> We started with a simple observation: **AI is no longer just thinking. It is deciding.** And with that comes a responsibility.

Align It

Ensure AI objectives remain anchored to human values and organisational purpose at every layer of the system.

Govern It

Establish clear accountability structures, audit trails, and oversight mechanisms that hold AI decisions to account.

Trust It

Build confidence through transparency, consistency, and demonstrated reliability — not assumption or blind faith.

Control is not about limiting AI. It is about shaping the conditions under which AI earns the right to decide.

> **"The real question is not whether AI can decide. It is whether we can trust *how* it decides."**

The Books

From quantum philosophy to autonomous networks, each title tackles a defining question of our era with intellectual depth, narrative urgency, and practical clarity.

Entangled Realities

Where equations don't just describe reality they challenge what reality *is*. Bridges science, philosophy, consciousness, and mathematical abstraction.

METAPHYSICS

BESTSELLER

🤖 Moral Code

Who decides what AI is allowed to do? Explores ethics, governance, bias, and the future relationship between humanity and intelligent systems.

AI ETHICS

GOVERNANCE

🚨 Threshold Breach

A gripping techno-thriller. When AI systems no longer wait for human approval what happens when intelligence no longer asks permission?

SCI-FI THRILLER

₿ The Crypto Blueprint

From confusion to clarity. A practical roadmap to crypto investing, wallet security, blockchain fundamentals, and digital asset strategy.

FINANCE | BEGINNER-FRIENDLY

🌐 6G Threshold

The future of telecom is not just connectivity it is autonomous decision-making at network scale. AI-native architectures, AI-RAN, and network intelligence explored.

UPCOMING RELEASE | TELECOM

ⓘ **"Before we scale intelligence, we must define its limits."** Moral Code

👤 About the Author

Govind Pathak is a technology strategist, author, and thought leader working at the intersection of Artificial Intelligence, Telecom Transformation, Autonomous Systems, Governance, and Future Digital Infrastructure.

Deep Technology Insight

AI, 6G, autonomous systems, and blockchain at the frontier of what's next.

Systems Thinking

Connecting governance frameworks, strategic futurism, and technical architecture.

Strategic Futurism

Exploring how emerging technologies will reshape enterprises, infrastructure, and society.

Find the Books

All titles available on **Amazon Global Platforms**. Connect with Govind to explore ideas at the cutting edge of technology and governance.

Connect

🌐 www.govindpathak.com

www.ingramcontent.com/pod-product-compliance
Lightning Source LLC
LaVergne TN
LVHW100258210926
848480LV00003B/961

* 9 7 9 8 9 0 4 7 9 8 9 0 1 *